Advance Praise for *Talking Back to Facebook*

"Steyer has penned a vital wake-up call for parents and government. He is a champion of both kids and the digital revolution. But he's neither giddy nor an apologist. He recognizes that companies like Facebook and Google and video game makers sway our kids, how they think and read and study and behave. If you're a parent and want some shrewd tips on parenting in this digital age and how to protect your children, read this book."

—Ken Auletta, author of *Googled: The End of the World as We Know It*

"In this courageous book, Jim Steyer pulls no punches. Whether or not you agree with his critique of Facebook and its Silicon Valley siblings, you must grapple with the deep issues that he raises."

—Howard Gardner, Hobbs Professor of Cognition and Education, Harvard Graduate School of Education

"Jim Steyer is a relentless advocate for kids. Focusing on how the media intersects with their lives, Jim boldly takes on the issues, exploring the good, the bad, and the ugly alike—always the first to begin the conversation. I urge every parent to read this book so that we can be prepared to navigate how new forms of media and communication are transforming children's lives."

—Cyma Zarghami, president, Nickelodeon Group

"Smart, savvy, sophisticated, down-to-earth. A book that parents and children can read together. A conversation starter for families."

—Sherry Turkle, author of *Alone Together*

Also by James P. Steyer

The Other Parent

TALKING BACK TO
FACEBOOK

The Common Sense Guide
to Raising Kids in the Digital Age

James P. Steyer

with a foreword by

Chelsea Clinton

Scribner

New York   London   Toronto   Sydney   New Delhi

Scribner
A Division of Simon & Schuster, Inc.
1230 Avenue of the Americas
New York, NY 10020

First Scribner trade paperback edition May 2012

SCRIBNER and design are registered trademarks of The Gale Group, Inc., used under
license by Simon & Schuster, Inc., the publisher of this work.

For information about special discounts for bulk purchases,
please contact Simon & Schuster Special Sales at
1-866-506-1949 or business@simonandschuster.com.

The Simon & Schuster Speakers Bureau can bring authors to your live event.
For more information or to book an event contact the Simon & Schuster Speakers
Bureau at 1-866-248-3049 or visit our website at www.simonspeakers.com.

Designed by Carla Jayne Jones

Manufactured in the United States of America

3   5   7   9   10   8   6   4   2

Library of Congress Control Number: 2012007165

ISBN: 978-1-4516-5811-8
ISBN: 978-1-4516-5734-0 (pbk)
ISBN: 978-1-4516-5735-7 (ebook)

To my kids: Lily, Kirk, Carly, and Jesse.
You were the reason that I wrote this book,
and you mean more to me than anything. . . .
And fortunately, each of you certainly has learned
how to Talk Back to Your Dad.

Contents

Part I
The RAP on Digital Media:
Relationships, Attention/Addiction, and Privacy

Contents

Part II
Parenting 2.0: Top Common Sense Tips

Foreword by Chelsea Clinton

When I was little—well, until I went to college—my parents had clear guidelines about media consumption, like their rules against sugary cereal and allowing pizza only on weekends. When I was in elementary school, my parents let me watch thirty minutes of television a day, with unlimited cartoon viewing on Saturday mornings. When I was a teenager, I secured precious permission to watch *ER,* even though each episode was twice as long as my daily allotment. We saw lots of movies as a family, listened to the radio in the car to and from school, soccer practice, and ballet, and, after my parents (or maybe it was Santa) gave me a Commodore computer for Christmas in 1987, I played the Carmen San Diego and Oregon Trail games, generally with my dad beside me, for hundreds of hours.

In our house, media had its place. With the exception of an Arkansas football game, we did not watch television or listen to the radio during meals, and media consumption, like meals, was a shared family experience. As we had dinner together, we frequently talked about the media in and surrounding our lives. My parents always asked me what I thought about the television shows, movies, music, and computer games

I was consuming with them and, less commonly, by myself or with friends. The earliest conversation like this that I remember was about *Snow White Live*, when I was about five years old. The most painful one I remember was when I confessed I had watched *Dirty Dancing* at a friend's house—I was eight or nine and PG-13 movies were explicitly off-limits. My parents were disappointed, and knowing that was far worse than any punishment they could mete out—though I think I was grounded for a weekend, too.

Growing up, I knew that it was important to talk to my parents about what I was hearing, seeing, and reading—and how it made me feel—and about what I was not watching, not listening to, and not participating in, even if my friends sometimes were.

During meals, my parents and I also talked about the media surrounding our lives—what was written in the local papers and what local TV stations were saying about our family. Sometimes my parents would start the conversations; sometimes I would, prompted by something I had read in the morning paper or something someone had said to me at school. What was true in a given story? What wasn't true? Why did the truth sometimes not seem to matter? Those conversations helped me develop a broad and healthy skepticism about the media, as well as a respect for its ability—in a news story, song, computer game, or movie—to empower or disempower people. By the time I was in junior high school, I realized that it was important to understand a given media report's intent, message, and interests, whether political, profit, or something else altogether. Our talks over breakfast and dinner also strengthened my relationship with my parents. If we could talk about the good, the bad, and the ugly in the media—whether it related to our family or to a fictional television or movie narrative—we could talk about anything in our own lives. In other words, talking about the media helped foster an honest and open relationship between my parents and me. That honesty in our conversations continues to this day.

One thing my parents and I didn't talk about when I was little, however, was how the media could impact or influence privacy for everyone, including kids. Given the persistent media interest in our lives in Little Rock, in Washington, and today, we certainly talked about privacy. However, we did not talk about the ways in which social media and technology would enable kids and adults to give up their privacy before they fully understand what privacy is, why it's important, and the implications of leading a life in which privacy, online or off, doesn't exist. Facebook and Twitter had not yet been imagined, and there was no such thing as an online identity.

Today, many kids are spending more time consuming media than interacting with their parents or teachers, and the challenges are vast—from the many young people who regret by high school what they've already posted about themselves to cyberbullying, to the hypersexualization of female characters in video games to the "ratings creep" in the movies and music kids consume. (Movies today contain significantly more sex and violence, on average, than movies with the same rating ten or twenty years ago.)

In *Talking Back to Facebook*, Jim Steyer explains how his family navigates these challenges—and opportunities—plainly and respectfully. He also explains how every family can mediate traditional and digital media in their kids' lives so it doesn't control them, and how they can help their kids grow into responsible, respectful digital citizens. Thankfully, the strategies Jim articulates are not esoteric—they're specific and practical, even if not always easy, for kids and their parents.

I first met Jim when I took one of his classes as a college sophomore. I then took another of his classes, became his teaching assistant, and was his research assistant for his first book, *The Other Parent*. Later, I proudly joined the board of Common Sense Media, the organization Jim started to better educate and equip parents to make the right media choices for their kids' mental, physical, and developmental health. There are many things I respect and admire about Jim, none more than his commitment to his family and to helping families everywhere help their kids grow up in a way that is safe, secure, and fun. His—and Common Sense Media's—ultimate aim is to ensure that media plays an empowering, supportive role in kids' learning and development, but isn't the main character in any kid's story. *Talking Back to Facebook* is Jim's most recent effort to do just that—to help parents and future parents (including, hopefully, Marc and me) in the twenty-first century best help kids to write their own stories, star in their own movies, discover their own dreams, and grow up to be the people they aspire to be, regardless of the most popular app, Facebook page, game, movie, or song in a given moment.

Introduction

I t's 6:30 p.m.—dinnertime at our house—and food's on the table. I call seven-year-old Jesse, who's out on the street riding his bike, and he slowly strolls in with a big grin on his face.

"Hey, Dad," he says, "can I borrow your iPhone after dinner so I can play that bowling game on it for ten minutes?"

I laugh. He knows the answer, but he's asking anyway.

I start rounding up our other three kids. Carly, fourteen, is in the living room, bopping her head rhythmically while she listens to music on her iPod. I stand in front of her, loudly intoning—to penetrate her earbuds—that it's time for dinner.

"Just a sec, Dad," she says, nodding her head. "Lemme finish this song."

I have no idea what she's listening to, and I still haven't seen our seventeen-year-old, Kirk, but I know where I'll find him. I walk into the family room, where Kirk is glued to the big-screen TV, clutching his Xbox controller and playing his favorite video game, FIFA Soccer.

"Kirk," I tell him, "dinner's ready."

"Can't I finish the game, Dad?" he begs. "Just a few more minutes."

"Nope! That's enough video games for today. You've hit your one-hour limit. It's time for dinner, now! But after that," I say, "why don't we toss the baseball outside? I'd like to see that new curveball you've been talking about."

He grunts, switches off his controller, and mutters a few monosyllables as he follows me to the dinner table. The other kids are already sitting down, including Lily, who just graduated from high school.

"Hey, Daddy, how was your day? Can I borrow the car tonight?" she asks, sticking her cell phone in her shirt pocket. "I just saw on Facebook that there's a party, and all my friends are going." She gives me that adorable grin that always works.

My wife, Liz, and I smile at each other. We're glad to have all the kids at home for a family dinner. We try to eat together at least four or five times a week. All phones and devices are strictly banned at the dinner table, parents' included. It's an important ritual: forty-five minutes or so of completely unplugged, screen-free time in a family life that's overflowing with digital media. Like most kids today, Lily, Kirk, Carly, and Jesse live much of their lives in a digital world. Technology is their native language, and as devices converge and become more capable and mobile, they're using them—far more easily than Liz and I—to connect, create, and communicate constantly, from almost anywhere, about virtually everything.

As parents, where do we draw the line? How do we balance the obvious benefits of computers and other digital technology with the growing risks of addiction, distraction, loss of innocence, and lack of privacy? With our kids' digital reality changing so fast, how do we even know what they're being exposed to, what we should worry about, and what common sense rules we should set?

Personally, new digital technology often seems overwhelming to me. I feel like I'm always playing catch-up, even though it's my job as founder and CEO of Common Sense Media, the nation's leading authority on the effects of media and technology on kids. The more I speak to education and child development experts and thousands of fellow parents and teachers around the country, the more I'm moved by the enormity of the changes occurring before our eyes with so little discussion and under-standing of their impact on kids and society.

What's at Stake for Childhood and Adolescence

Howard Gardner of the Harvard Graduate School of Education, who developed the idea of multiple intelligences, calls this an "epochal change." He compares the revolution in digital media to the invention of the printing press because of its extraordinary impact on the way we communicate, share information, and interact with other human beings. It's hard to believe that the biggest technology challenge parents faced in 1990 was controlling their kids' use of telephone *landlines*. Boy, have things changed, and our kids' social, emotional, and cognitive develop-ment skills have been profoundly affected. At times, it seems like they're subjects of a vast, uncontrolled social experiment. And it's an experiment that has dramatic implications for our notions of childhood, learning, and human relationships. As parents and educators, we have to engage with this new reality and influence it, as well as our kids, in healthy, responsible ways.

The fact is, kids are thrown into this brave new world from the day they're born. When parents post cute pictures of their babies in adorable outfits and poses, they're creating the first outlines of their kids' digital footprint. By the time they're two, more than 90 percent of all children have an online history, and many have figured out how to take pictures and watch cartoons on their parents' smartphones. At five, many are typ-ing on a computer keyboard and downloading and playing games on cell phones and tablet computers. I clearly remember the day when our daughter Carly, at age six, "Googled" herself for the first time.

By seven or eight, some kids have phones of their own, and they're playing in virtual worlds and staring at screens when they're together with friends. At ten or eleven, they're downloading and streaming Web content, playing online games like World of Warcraft, and begging for smartphones and Facebook accounts. By twelve or thirteen, most kids

3

have Facebook pages—with or without their parents' permission. They're using technology in the classroom and texting friends or Facebooking them instead of talking to them in person. Kids are getting online at home, at friends' houses, at the library, and on the bus. As they become teens, they fully inhabit a virtual world with online and offline identities and special languages, social rules, and relationships—usually with no adult supervision. They're performing, creating, and posing for invisible audiences—often unaware that, even when they change and mature, their online errors of judgment and personal postings might not go away. There's no "eraser" button, and the consequences of youthful mistakes can be enormously painful.

For the past five years, I've been witnessing how social networks, especially Facebook, have transformed the lives of my students at Stanford University, where I teach classes on civil rights, civil liberties, and children's issues. The technology has literally changed the way people relate to each other, get together, and present their image to the world. Interestingly, when I polled my class recently, more than half of my students said they wished Facebook didn't exist. Several of them said they didn't like the way it drained so much of their time and affected their interactions with friends and peers. Many told me that Facebook can diminish the quality and depth of personal relationships and weaken their basic communications skills. But, of course, they *had* to be on it, they said, because everyone else was.

Facebook, the world's largest social network site, was cofounded by Mark Zuckerberg and his Harvard friend Eduardo Saverin in 2004. It started out as a social networking tool designed exclusively for students at Harvard, but it quickly spread to students at other elite universities like Stanford, Yale, and Columbia. Soon after, Facebook expanded to hundreds of colleges across the nation, demonstrating the extraordinary, viral nature of the Web, especially social networks. In 2005, Facebook opened its site to high school students, and the following year, it welcomed a fast-growing number of adults.

Like other social network sites, Facebook basically operates as a system of interconnected personal profiles—essentially easily customized personal homepages, for which even technological Luddites can choose profile pictures and add many more photos, "status updates," and personal information. In addition, Facebook users can also comment on each other's photos and click the "Like" button on a particular image, post, or Web page if they want to give it an electronic "thumbs-up." The problems come when vulnerable youngsters define themselves by the "Like" button or when comments about photos turn mean, cruel, and hateful, as they often do.

Personally, I think social media sites like Facebook and Google Plus are great ways to connect and stay in touch with old and new friends. I know a lot more about the lives of my old high school buddies, for example, now that many of them have contacted me on Facebook. I've also seen how LinkedIn has been a source of great professional connections for friends and colleagues, who use it to stay in touch with work associates, find employment opportunities, and recruit job candidates. Along with Craigslist, LinkedIn has helped revolutionize the hiring process.

But the truth is, kids use social networks differently from adults, in ways that can be hurtful and unhealthy. My eighteen-year-old daughter, Lily, for example, rolls her eyes when grown-ups talk about the positive social experiences they have on Facebook. "When kids go on Facebook," Lily explains, "it's a completely different experience—you have no idea." Instead of using Facebook and other social networks to strengthen face-to-face relationships, she says, many kids, especially teens, use them *instead* of real human-to-human interactions. Posting and text messaging are quick, efficient, cold ways to communicate, especially when you don't have to be sensitive to the emotional nuances of facial expressions and tone of voice. But these new forms of electronic communication can also be cruel and damaging, and anonymous online communities can instantly amplify the impact and pain of bullying, gossip, and social exclusion.

One fifteen-year-old girl at a school near our home committed suicide after she discovered, via Facebook, that she hadn't been invited to a slumber party. That's a tragic and extreme case, but kids in every town, every day, witness or suffer from cyberbullying. With popular apps like

Honesty Box, which allow users to send anonymous, untraceable messages, many kids feel empowered to post anything to and about anyone, no matter how hurtful or untrue. Other top apps, like Compare People, encourage kids to compare and rank themselves in dozens of sensitive categories—like cutest, sexiest, and smartest—against other kids in their social network. And teens build massive "friend lists" on Facebook or "followers" on Twitter to assess and compare their popularity. At a stage of life when peer acceptance is absolutely vital and self-esteem can be very fragile, these impersonal digital tools are often abused, with consequences that can be harmful for millions and tragic for a few.

I've been trying to get a handle on what Facebook truly means for kids and the broader society ever since 2007, when I met Mark Zuckerberg at a conference at Google. Today, Facebook is the giant, eight-hundred-pound gorilla of social media. It claims nearly a billion members worldwide, up from only a few million six years ago. It is now the top-visited website in the United States, surpassing Google, and it's literally revolutionizing the way young people communicate, build relationships, and express their identities—with virtually no thoughtful analysis of its impact. If Facebook were a country, it would be the world's third largest in population, trailing only China and India. And just like those other emerging global giants, we ignore its growth and power at our own risk.

I decided to call this book *Talking Back to Facebook* for two reasons. First, Facebook, to me, is the most potent symbol of the digital revolution and the way it's impacting kids and teens. Second, many of the parents and teachers I encountered while researching this book told me how helpless they feel dealing with Facebook and the onslaught of 24/7 digital reality that it represents. They feel isolated in their concerns about how social networks are affecting their kids' way of relating to themselves and others, and they feel overwhelmed and powerless to do anything about it. The speed of change has simply been so rapid that they didn't see these changes coming, and they feel blindsided by the impact.

But parents have the right—indeed, the obligation—to speak up and be heard. They have the right and the responsibility to assert control over how they raise their kids and about new technology platforms that are playing such a powerful role in their children's lives. I wrote *Talking Back to Facebook* to empower parents, first and foremost, as well as teachers and young people. The purpose of this book is to give you some of the basic knowledge and information you need to understand what's going on, as well as a voice in determining the impact on your own kids and our broader culture. Parenting can and *does* make a huge difference in kids' lives—and informed, common sense parenting is absolutely essential in this dizzying new digital age.

The issues, of course, are far bigger than Facebook and other social media. There are now approximately 2 billion Internet users across the globe, and more than 5 billion people own cell phones. The implications of this connectivity are simply mind-boggling. According to a recent Nielsen study, the average thirteen- to seventeen-year-old now exchanges 3,339 text messages a month; that's about 111 *a day*.[1] But their phones aren't just for texting and occasional phone calls. Young people also use them for listening to music, filming videos, snapping and sharing photos, and going online. Sure, they use their computers to do homework. But they also use them to socialize, stream video, and create movies and songs. They're not just watching TV, listening to iPods, and playing video games. They're inhabiting a virtual universe that's shaping their reality, setting their expectations, guiding their behavior, and defining their interests, choices, and values.

Whether we like it or not, kids are now spending far more time with media and technology than they are with their families or in school. Clocking in at nearly eight hours a day on average (or nearly eleven hours per day when you include multitasking), that's more time than they spend doing any other single activity.[2] What messages about life are they absorbing? Whose messages are they listening to? What are they seeing and learning? And what do we know about the impact on their development and social and emotional health?

We may think of our kids' online, mobile, and technological activities as their "digital lives." But to them, their plugged-in, networked world *is* life. It's displacing and replacing the real, physical world of interaction and communication that's always been the core human experience. I was recently in a room with three twelve-year-old girls who were sitting on a couch just inches away from one another. Although they were having a conversation, they weren't talking to each other. They were texting. They made no eye contact and never glimpsed one another's expressions or body language. Instead, they sat there staring at their smartphones, fingers flying, exchanging digital messages. That shift from face-to-face to digital communication is an enormous change, and we haven't even begun to fully understand, or to conduct research on, its enormous impact on kids and society.

Make no mistake. This is a huge change that's occurring at warp speed. When most of us were tweens and teens, we weren't sharing details of our personal lives with a vast, invisible, online audience. We weren't constantly distracted and interrupted by text messages and IMs in the middle of school, homework, and face-to-face conversations. If we did have computers, they were usually tethered to a table or a desk; they had physical boundaries and didn't go everywhere with us like they do now, in the form of powerful mobile phones—pocket-size minicomputers— that let kids access online information wherever they go. Our parents could protect us, to some extent, by controlling our access—like keeping kids out of the deep end of the pool until they're strong enough swimmers. But now, digital media and technology are everywhere; even Mount Everest has 3G phone service. Cell phones enable kids to jump on the Internet and go anywhere, from anywhere, at any time—often without their parents' knowledge or supervision. Instead of staying in the safe end of the pool, children and teens today are swimming in a vast ocean of information and media impressions. Because we can't always keep them out of dangerous waters, it's more important than ever to give them the skills they need to navigate, play, and explore safely, and to stay afloat.

The RAP on Kids and Digital Media

The risks of the new digital reality are related to a cluster of digital media issues that I call RAP—relationships, attention/addiction problems, and privacy. These three related concerns are having a fundamental effect on the nature of childhood and on all of us. We will explore these issues at length in the following chapters, but I will preview them here.

Relationships

The new digital media is altering the basic ways we relate to one another as friends and family, transforming the experience of human connection. Technology is becoming the architect of a new intimacy.

Think about it. How often in the past week have you seen kids or adults walking around with their attention fixated on a cell phone, or sitting on a sofa with their eyes glued to a laptop, iPad, or TV screen? Focused on a device or a computer screen for seemingly hours on end, people can ignore meaningful personal connections and emotional cues. Parents often can drive kids crazy with their lack of genuine attention, and vice versa. I must admit that it sometimes happens in my own home. Leading child development experts such as Sherry Turkle, professor of the social studies of science and technology at MIT, believe that digital media affects our ability to give full, undistracted attention to each other and our own thoughts. The lack of disconnected downtime in our tech-dominated lives is disrupting our ties to each other and adding significant emotional stress to the lives of millions of kids and adults.

We're also witnessing the rise of new forms of damaging, destructive interpersonal behavior, like cyberbullying, that are facilitated by digital platforms. It's a lot easier to say or do something truly hurtful to someone else, without considering the consequences, when it requires only a few keystrokes on a computer or cell phone.

Attention/Addiction

Attention deficit issues are also becoming a huge concern for educators and psychologists. Many experts and parents worry that kids are becoming less able to focus well in the distracting world of digital media. Some believe these devices are creating a whole new generation of youngsters with more problems related to attention and concentration. Leading pediatricians, brain researchers, and child health experts, including Dr.

Dimitri Christakis at the University of Washington, note that attention-deficit hyperactivity disorder (ADHD)—characterized by abnormal levels of distractedness, impulsiveness, and overactivity—has become ten times more common in children in the past two to three decades, and they link this spike to the overstimulation of developing brains by digital media.

It's distressing to see your kids try to focus on homework when they're being pinged every few minutes by incoming texts, Facebook notifications, and instant messages. Even at a top-flight university like Stanford, I see the impact of this constant distraction in the classroom. During class, many of my students used to routinely check their e-mails and Facebook pages—until I banned the use of laptops during my lectures. Many of today's students are less able to concentrate, write well, think coherently, and synthesize information than they were just a few years ago. And every year they seem to have shallower and shorter attention spans, as well as diminished memory capacity. The reason, according to David Meyer, psychology professor in the University of Michigan's Cognition and Perception Program, is that multitasking causes a kind of "mental brownout." The brain just doesn't have enough processing power to do several things simultaneously, so the lights start dimming and performance suffers.

Digital media can also be addictive, and I've learned about that personally from my son Kirk. If we permitted it, Kirk would probably spend countless hours playing ultraviolent video games like Call of Duty or Assassin's Creed—sitting like a brainless zombie in front of an Xbox, computer, or TV screen, blowing enemies' heads off in brutal, bloody virtual worlds. And if he wasn't doing that, he'd be happy to spend hours Facebooking his friends instead of getting together with them or going outside to play baseball or ride his bike in the neighborhood. Too often, I've had to stand right in front of him and block his view of a screen to get his attention.

I should add that Kirk, seventeen, is really smart and an accomplished athlete. But for Kirk, like many other kids, video games and social networks are more than a pastime. They're a compulsion, a consuming adrenaline rush that can crowd out other aspects of a healthy life. They don't just waste time, they steal it in large chunks—from homework, from being outside and physically active, and from communicating and interacting with friends and family in a meaningful way.

To deal with these worries, my wife, Liz, and I keep strict limits on Kirk's gaming and his use of Facebook, cell phones, and other digital media. But it's a constant battle, especially now that he's an older teenager and more independent. Clearly, our family is not immune to these challenges, even though I spend my days trying to make video game manufacturers accountable for selling ultraviolent and hypersexualized games to kids and urging Facebook and other tech giants to act more responsibly when it comes to young people, especially regarding the increasingly serious issue of privacy.

Privacy

Privacy, in particular, is a hugely important and explosive issue. Online interactions that kids think are just between good friends may very well be seen by many more people than they intend. And since kids don't always think twice before they self-reveal, they often "overshare"—leaving embarrassing digital footprints that could someday damage their reputations. The consequences of this potentially fundamental shift in privacy norms during the past few years are difficult to overstate. As leading child development experts observe, what is intimacy without privacy? And what are the implications for healthy identity formation when so much is played out on a public technology platform where there are huge social pressures to project an idealized image? In this digital hall of mirrors, where every action or posting is designed to get a reaction, self-esteem, narcissism, anxiety, and authenticity are big issues for vulnerable preteens and teens. Without clear digital privacy boundaries, millions of kids and adults face a world where humiliating data and images persist forever, and there are no second chances to delete embarrassing mistakes. When you consider the very real threats of cyberbullying and sexting, it's clear that all teens need to learn to self-reflect before they self-reveal.

Kids' privacy is also being breached by advertisers and marketers, who now routinely target kids with unwanted ads and personal messages tailored to their online profiles. In addition, many sites like Foursquare or

Loopt reveal kids' exact geographical location—at stores or coffeeshops, for instance—without their clear knowledge or permission. As the parent of three teenagers, these geolocation services trouble me deeply; this isn't a minor business practice that society should permit without robust public debate as well as new laws regulating privacy.

Unfortunately, in today's Wild West digital media environment, our current privacy laws and regulatory oversight are totally out of date. The most recent privacy statute protecting children was written in 1998, the Middle Ages in the history of the Internet. The last time we seriously examined our nation's privacy laws, Facebook founder Mark Zuckerberg was still in grade school, and YouTube, text messaging, and Twitter didn't exist. Today, in a world where people can post and say literally anything about themselves or others—often anonymously and in many cases without permission—our whole notion of privacy is being transformed, with significant, long-term consequences for the future.

As a society, we cannot mutely shrug our shoulders as Silicon Valley companies hurtle forward, introducing new privacy-threatening products for personal gain. With precious little analysis, let alone meaningful, rational discourse, self-anointed "tech gurus," fixated on efficiently accumulating data, act as though long-held privacy norms are no longer relevant to the average person or family. "Just deal with it, dude," seems to be their response.

The privacy genie may be out of the bottle in some respects, but the debate is just getting started, and the implications for kids are transformational. The stakes are too high, and the consequences too enormous, for Americans to continue to sit passively by. Privacy is a matter that affects all of us, especially children and teens, and we all need to get educated and involved in order to protect it.

A New Reality for Families

In his seminal 1985 book about television, *Amusing Ourselves to Death,* the late media observer Neil Postman called childhood a "sequence of revealed secrets." It used to be, kids were protected from information they weren't ready to understand. That innocence was once considered priceless, an essential element of childhood and growing up. But today, when unfiltered messages bombard our kids from every angle—on Facebook, cell phones, games, advertisements, the Internet, TV, and movies—gatekeeping is difficult or nearly impossible, especially for older kids. Information simply outraces our ability to control it, and we've lost our ability to control our kids' exposure to knowledge.

For parents and teachers, the easy, unfiltered access to information and images can be a shock. I met a father in Omaha who told me about an uncomfortable situation he'd recently had with his eleven-year-old daughter. He had asked her to look up some information for him on the Internet, but after a few minutes, she screamed, "Oh my God, Dad, look at this!" She had mistakenly clicked on a pornographic website and was staring at some bizarre sexual images and scenes he could never have imagined, even as a forty-year-old man. "What do you do when that happens?" he asked me. "How do you shield your child from too much information, way too soon?"

As parents, our instinct is to protect our kids and control their environment, but digital technology makes that almost impossible. That's the reality. We can't change it, and we can't go back. But we can, and we must, help kids navigate this new environment safely so they don't get lost or hurt. We have to teach them to understand the media messages they receive and how to use the technology platforms at their fingertips in responsible, productive ways. We can't shield kids completely from all the images and messages that confront them, so it's vital to give them the tools and values to help filter those messages successfully and to make good, common sense judgments. We can limit their access and exposure to traditional and digital media, especially when they're young. We can help them process and understand media messages and content. And we can use media and technology in our homes and schools in positive ways that help kids make the most of the extraordinary creative and learning opportunities that technology makes possible.

Equally as important, we can and must join together as parents and citizens to discuss the broader implications of digital technology, instead of standing by as it transforms our lives. We must examine the impact that Facebook and other social network platforms have on how kids communicate and relate to each other. We must insist upon funding research on topics like addiction and ADHD, which are related to the constant use and overuse of digital media. And we must demand new privacy laws in this nation, so that we can restore the critically important concept of personal privacy in young people's lives, as well as our own.

Perils and Possibilities

As media and technology evolve at a dizzying pace, they're creating a host of new dangers and opportunities. As we discussed, digital technology threatens the quality of relationships, creates attention and addiction problems, and can invade our kids' privacy. On the positive side, there are remarkable new opportunities for creativity, collaboration, and connectedness. Kids can literally access the world at their fingertips. For school, they can search and learn about virtually anything that fascinates them. A sixth-grader I know, for instance, taught himself how to play killer lead guitar by watching how-to videos on YouTube. And thanks to digital media, kids now have countless ways to share their talents and passions. The collaboration skills they pick up on social network sites, such as how to create communities of people with common interests, can also serve them well at every age, provided they use them wisely. And new technology is transforming education in positive ways— providing exciting, accessible ways to deliver and enhance educational content with photos, videos, and immersive technology. In one sense, there are more possibilities than ever for kids to learn, create, express, and interact. The opportunities for twenty-first-century education are breathtaking, and they represent a central focus of our work at Common Sense Media.

Kids haven't changed. They're still exploring and discovering who they are, just as we did when we were growing up. They're still searching for acceptance and experimenting with risky behavior. What *has* changed is that there's now a permanent record of their explorations, with implications that nobody can predict and that none of us can effectively control.

Parenting Hasn't Changed

For parents, this new world can seem overwhelming. Many kids understand and use these new devices and platforms better than we do. Their technological abilities, however, frequently eclipse their emotional maturity and good judgment. Unrestricted access to information and people can result in age-inappropriate contact as well as totally inappropriate content. It's our responsibility as parents to help our kids make good choices online. We can't protect our kids from all the possible dangers, but we can help them grow up with the judgment and critical-thinking skills they need to protect themselves as responsible and safe digital citizens.

In our twenty-first-century economy, most parents realize that it's now as important for their kids to know how to use digital media responsibly as it is to learn traditional skills like reading and writing. Research makes clear that most parents and educators see lots of positive benefits from the new technology. But just as kids need to learn how to swim, eat properly, and drive a car, they need to know how to live in the digital world safely and ethically. It's still up to parents and teachers to guide kids—to teach them strong values and good judgment and how to make proper decisions. We all need to know the new "rules of the road" for the digital age.

Navigating these challenges can be scary, but that doesn't mean we have to fear new media and technology, overreact, or forbid their use. What this new reality ultimately requires is simple common sense. To help, Common Sense Media and others have developed new curricula and tools for "Digital Literacy" and "Digital Citizenship" that can help every child learn how to be safe, smart, and responsible in the digital world. They are now available to every school and home in the United States.[3]

The bottom line is clear. We need to know what's happening in our kids' digital lives, talk with them about what they're seeing and experiencing, and teach them to think critically about the images and messages they encounter. We need to limit their access to certain media and technology, starting when they're very young. And we have to stay involved in how they process messages and images as they gain independence.

The good news is that this kind of parental involvement has a really positive effect. Research shows that it can make a huge difference in the amount of media that kids consume. That's important, because studies have shown that kids who spend less time with media have far better grades in school and higher levels of personal contentment.

We know what parents and educators can do to help kids navigate new media safely. The tips in this book won't guarantee that you'll avoid issues and conflicts. My son Kirk, for instance, frequently reminds me that I'm his "worst nightmare" as a parent. But this book will give you practical, common sense tools for raising and educating your kids in the mobile, socially networked digital world.

You, of course, are the ultimate expert when it comes to your own children. Only you can make the judgment call about what's right or age appropriate—when it's okay for your child to e-mail, text, have a cell phone or a Facebook page, download a song with explicit lyrics, or see a PG-13 movie. But *Talking Back to Facebook* will hopefully help you think about the implications of the new technology and make those calls.

This book is divided into two sections. The first part will give you an overview of the issues related to digital media and kids and the background to understand what's happening and why. The second part of the book gives you simple tips and guidance, for kids from birth through age fifteen, to help you and your family make good decisions about parenting and educating kids in a digital world. If you're wondering if your two-year-old should play games on your iPad, or if you've just discovered that your eleven-year-old has been looking at X-rated websites, this book can help you keep your kid safe, secure, and ready to reap the powerful benefits of digital media. Perhaps most important, I also hope this book will help launch a national dialogue about what we as a society can do to minimize the perils and maximize the profound possibilities of this extraordinary new digital age.

Part I

The RAP on Digital Media: Relationships, Attention/ Addiction, and Privacy

Chapter One

Relationships: Connection, Intimacy, and Self-Image

Our infatuation with technology provides
an easy alternative to love.[1]
—Jonathan Franzen

We all know the following experience. You walk into your kid's room to have a conversation and she simply ignores you, glued to the computer or TV screen in front of her. Maybe she looks up and mutters, "Yeah, Dad. Hold on a sec," then turns back to the glowing screen or device.

Or there's the conversation with your friend: you stand in front of him, talking about an important work relationship, or maybe some ideas about where to have dinner. He nods but doesn't bother to meet your eyes, because he's staring down at his iPhone or CrackBerry. Worse, he starts texting right in the middle of your conversation, like that's accepted social etiquette these days.

This is the culture of i-Distraction. It can be very rude and often ignores basic social courtesies. According to experts, it's also eroding the quality of interpersonal relationships with friends, family members, and coworkers. Increasing attachment to technology means decreasing attention to human beings—and the biggest losers are unquestionably kids and parents.

Paying attention to another person is a basic sign of how much you care about them. When you're not paying attention, you're sending the opposite message. Stanford communications professor Clifford Nass recently told me a powerful story that drove home that point. At the undergraduate dorm where he lives as a resident fellow, a female student, visibly in tears, was talking to a close girlfriend about a difficult personal problem she was having. She was clearly upset. While she was speaking, her friend had a laptop open and kept glancing at it frequently while she listened to the whole tearful story.[2] The distraught student was aware that her friend was distracted but seemed to accept the latter's rudeness. It was an example to Nass of how digital distraction reduces compassion and empathy, even in direct, one-on-one conversations. If you're not paying full attention to another person, you may hear their words, but you're very likely to miss key emotional nuances, and your responses will be shallower because you aren't fully engaged.

Basic norms and relationships are being upended in a world of cell phones, laptops, iPads, and other digital distractions, which are increasingly isolating people in their own digital cocoons. MIT's Sherry Turkle, in her terrific book *Alone Together: Why We Expect More from Technology and Less from Each Other,*[3] observes that constant connectivity, in what seems like a paradoxical effect, seems to disrupt our attachments so much that we feel completely alone. Millions of people, for example—especially kids and teens—are increasingly connecting to other people only via text messages. This means that they don't have to look people in the eye or even hear their voices over the telephone. It may seem more efficient, but there also seems to be a connection between the frequent use of technology and the tendency of people to be less intimate and emotional in their human interactions.

At Stanford, Nass and his colleagues have been working on a study of nearly thirty-five hundred girls ages eight to twelve, looking at the relationship between their social well-being and their use of media versus face-to-face communication. They're examining everything from the girls' media multitasking, alone and with friends, to their use of texting and video games. These are crucial development years; research links girls' self-esteem at these ages to their later success and happiness in life. Nass's emerging research suggests that too much texting, Facebooking, and other online communication can be negatively associated with girls' social and emotional development.

One central problem is that text messages, instant messages, and online posts make it hard to read what the sender is really thinking and feeling. Without seeing and hearing the nuances of facial expression, body language, and tone of voice, kids can overinterpret digital messages, read meaning into posts, guess at the intent of the sender, and often misjudge it. Without the facial or vocal cues to make the meaning clear, a sarcastic comment may not come across well in a 160-character message and can be read as a literal statement that seems harsh or cruel. The irony is that online communication seems efficient, but because of the stripped-down, emotionless nature of digital messages, kids often spend a lot of time trying to read between the lines and pondering their meaning. Studies show that young people, in fact, feel greater insecurity and social anxiety in a world where text messaging and posting have become appropriate platforms for personal confessions, breakups, anger, and jealousy.

These trends carry enormous implications, especially for this generation of children and teens. When important emotional matters are crammed into technology spaces that are ill-suited for nuanced, complex feelings and honest engagement, human relationships can be profoundly affected.[4] In short, we may be potentially fostering a culture that is less attentive, compassionate, and caring, with less emotional intelligence.[5]

Many of the discussions I have had with other parents and teachers focus on how distracted and inattentive kids can become because of digital technology. The phenomenon, however, can also affect our own behavior as parents. That's one of the reasons my wife and I ban all media and digital devices from family meals. As most of us know, good role modeling is a critical aspect of parenting, so the best advice is to put the device down when your kids are around. Obviously, in this 24/7 wired world, parental self-discipline isn't always as easy to model as it should be, but I've heard poignant stories from kids who've grown up with parents distracted by digital media—pushing the playground swing with one hand, for example, while texting with the other, or keeping their eyes and ears glued to their phones at their kids' soccer games. A number of teens talked about parents texting while driving or interrupting long-planned family vacations because there wasn't an adequate Internet connection or mobile phone coverage at the hotel. They talked about parents texting during family dinners, making the excuse that "it's better than me being at the office."[6] Many kids have told me that they feel less loved and cared for by their "always on" parents. Preoccupied with omnipresent e-mail messages or clutching their phones, many parents unintentionally create walls between themselves and the children they love. The same, of course, is clearly true in reverse.[7]

The e-Personality and "The Culture of Me"

Digital media, some experts believe, may also have an important role in reshaping certain aspects of children's identities and personalities. Child development experts note that young people's tendency to develop their personalities on Facebook can be a major factor in what Sherry Turkle has termed "presentation anxiety." The process of constantly presenting your profile, likes, dislikes, and "relationship status" to the broader world can be emotionally stressful, especially for more vulnerable youngsters. Kids can experience deep insecurity as they try to create a perfect profile, choose the right pictures to post, and express the identity they want to present to their hundreds of Facebook "friends."[8] One of my younger teenage daughter's friends recently told me that she spent several painful hours trying to decide which music groups to list as her "favorites" on Facebook because she knew she would be heavily judged for the choices. Normal anxieties, which are part and parcel of childhood and adolescence, can be dramatically magnified.

24

Turkle and other leading psychologists are focusing attention on how teens' identities are formed and distorted through Facebook activities, texting, and online games. Needless to say, the pressure of creating public identities on Facebook does not encourage the risk-free opportunities for maturation that most teenagers need.[9] In a world of limitless connections and hundreds or even thousands of "friends," many relationships are bound to be shallow and unreal. As every parent and teacher knows, healthy relationships are core to a child's personal identity and development. But social networks and devices can often be a limiting factor in how people relate to one another emotionally and how much caring they exhibit in human social connections.

Even some of the original Internet visionaries have started waving red flags. Jaron Lanier, who is often credited with coining the term "virtual reality," has roundly criticized social network sites like Facebook and Twitter. In his recent book, *You Are Not a Gadget,* Lanier says they foster inauthentic, shallow interactions and asserts that teenagers are "driven more by fear than by love" to carefully maintain and update their online reputations.[10]

To me, it is also critically important to recognize that many millions of underage and emotionally vulnerable youngsters, many as young as ten or eleven, now spend hours each week on Facebook. The Children's Online Privacy Protection Act (COPPA) makes it illegal for companies to collect "personally identifiable" information—including name, phone number, e-mail or street address, and social security number—from children ages twelve and under without parental consent. That's why Facebook, like many other social networks, purports to exclude minors under thirteen. Despite that official stance, a recent study by *Consumer Reports* found that 7.5 million American kids under age thirteen are using the site.[11] As those of us who work in the kids' media field know, Facebook's age restrictions are essentially meaningless. Virtually anyone of any age can create a Facebook page with a false birth date or identity. The impact of social network practices on cognitive, social, and emotional development is magnified at such impressionable, vulnerable ages, especially because Facebook and other networks constantly encourage young users to "share" more and more information about their personal lives.

Some experts now believe that young people are also becoming increasingly impulse-driven and self-centered in the "all about me" world of constant status updates on Facebook and other social media platforms. Online, "all the world's a stage"; *you* are in the driver's seat, preening for a large audience of "friends" or followers. A number of astute social commentators have begun to criticize the self-absorbed nature of social media. As the author Jonathan Franzen recently wrote, "Our lives look a lot more interesting when they're filtered through the sexy Facebook interface. We star in our own movies, we photograph ourselves incessantly, we click the mouse and a machine confirms our sense of mastery. . . . We like the mirror and the mirror likes us. To friend a person is to merely include the person in our private hall of flattering mirrors."[12]

Stanford Medical School psychiatrist Elias Aboujaoude, author of *Virtually You: The Dangerous Powers of the E-Personality,* has observed that online behavior and personality formation seems to be bleeding into our lives offline. As Dr. Aboujaoude puts it, "We're becoming more impatient, more narcissistic, more regressed even when there is no browser in sight. Society starts to look like one big chat room, and we end up looking like avatars."[13] Researchers like Dr. Aboujaoude believe that these "e-personality" issues are more pronounced and problematic in kids because they're "digital natives"—the technology has always been part of their lives, and they're more susceptible to its influence. Some child development experts also believe that young people are exhibiting less social etiquette, politeness, and ethical behavior when they're online. Recent studies suggest these traits play out in activities such as compulsive buying, gambling, and casual hooking up. They can also been seen in impulsive texting and e-mailing, posting photos without thinking about the consequences, cyberbullying, and sexting.

Concerns about teen identity formation are hardly new. What *is* new for kids today is that so much of it is played out in public, and they can be criticized, even ostracized, for every mistake or uncool choice they make. That's a lot of risk and pressure at a very vulnerable time.

Facebook and Body Image

As the parent of two teenage girls growing up in an incredibly appearance-conscious culture, my concerns related to girls' body image have long been a subject of conversation in our home. When I was writing my first book, *The Other Parent,* more than ten years ago, I was keenly aware of the impact that media and entertainment messages have on body image, especially for girls and women. Those issues were first highlighted back in the 1970s in Jean Kilbourne's cutting-edge documentary *Killing Us Softly,* which my college girlfriend at first had to drag me to see. I was astounded by the enormity of the problem. More recently, I was interviewed for Jennifer Siebel Newsom's excellent new documentary film, *Miss Representation,* which highlights the many ways in which media continues to portray women and girls in demeaning, objectifying ways.

I hadn't really reflected a great deal on the impact of digital media, in particular Facebook, on girls' body image, however, until I began doing the research for this book. According to a study by Stanford's Cliff Nass, teen girls tend to present overly thin images of themselves on Facebook. In addition, the more concerned a girl is about her appearance, weight, and body image, the more she tends to check her Facebook profile and vice versa. The new research also shows that many teen girls Photoshop—digitally alter—their photos to appear thinner and carefully select photos for their Facebook profiles that make them look thinner, hoping to receive positive public feedback from their peers. At times, their focus on appearance and thinness verges on compulsion. With digital cameras on their mobile phones, many teen girls constantly monitor how photogenic they look, checking and rechecking their appearance in photos again and again.[14]

Many teen girls also comment incessantly on each other's appearance in Facebook photos—far more than they would in the real world, since they know that these displays of "friendship" are very public. Typical comments include "OMG! You're so gorgeous," or "Stop Being So Cute!," or "You are too hot, Sexxy Thing!" Indeed, some girls interviewed for an undergraduate thesis by a Common Sense colleague admitted asking their friends to make positive comments about their appearance in Facebook photos, in hopes that others would make similarly positive remarks.[15] Clearly, many of these girls use Facebook comments about their appearance as measuring sticks for friendship, self-image, and basic self-worth.

This cycle can have pernicious effects. By heightening the focus on their appearance, especially their weight, girls are constantly trying to appear thinner than they really are. This magnification effect of Facebook can, in some cases, be associated with eating disorders like anorexia or bulimia and other health-related issues. To date, the research on the relationship between social media and girls' appearance has tended to focus on objectification and self-harm. But there has also been growing criticism and analysis of pro-anorexia and pro-bulimia websites, which can teach visitors how to maintain or develop eating disorders.[16]

As the father of two teenage girls who deal with appearance pressures on a regular basis, I believe this is an issue that should be addressed in homes, classrooms, and public forums across the country, as often as possible. The main thing we can do as parents and educators is to place these issues firmly out in the open. In doing so, we can begin the necessary dialogue to educate all of our kids, and ourselves, about how to deal with these pressures in the increasingly public world of social media.

A young Common Sense Media staffer, Kelly Schryver, who's in her early twenties, recently summed up the issue of how social networks affect girls' body image:

"Thank God we didn't have Facebook when we were in middle school," a former classmate of mine recently expressed to me over dinner. On the one hand, it is crucial that we recognize Facebook's incredible potential to fortify girls' friendship and boost their self-esteem. Girls love staying in touch with friends they cannot see on a regular basis. They love looking at photos of one another. . . . On the other hand, we must also recognize that today's girls—for the first time—are growing up with mirrors that talk back to them. Girls not only use Facebook to check up on how they look, they also use it to gauge how others see them. Looking forward, we need to identify and question socially sanctioned online practices among girls that encourage them to self-objectify and . . . to help tomorrow's young women resist the urge to conflate self-worth, friendship, and physical attractiveness.[17]

Cyberbullying: How It Happens and Why It Hurts

As the parent of three teenagers, I've personally witnessed the pain and anguish of cyberbullying. Online, kids can say very hurtful things about other people anonymously, and they don't have to look them in the eye or see their reactions. In some instances, kids actually create fake identities in order to lure others into humiliating situations. For example, when Common Sense Media conducted focus groups among middle school students while developing our digital citizenship curriculum, we heard a story about a girl who pretended to be a classmate online. Using this joke persona, she made a boy in her class think she had a crush on him and lured him to a public rendezvous. When he got there, the whole class was there to laugh at him. She had told them all about her scheme, and a shocking number of kids showed up to witness it.

Of course, we've all heard even worse horror stories about cyberbullying in the national news over the past few years. Tragic cases—such as eighteen-year-old Rutgers student Tyler Clementi, who committed suicide after his roommate posted a video of him kissing another man, or the disturbing story of Phoebe Prince, a fifteen-year-old who took her own life after being constantly harassed on social networks and in school—have made millions aware of the extraordinary consequences of online bullying.

Cyberbullying, like all forms of bullying, is rooted in meanness and cruelty. What is different, however, is the anonymity factor, as well as the impersonal, impulsive nature of digital communication. These factors facilitate the cruelty of strangers and "friends" alike, which can range from slightly harmful teasing to more elaborate humiliations and physical threats. To be clear: social networks like Facebook or Google Plus or the text messaging capabilities on your kid's cell phone don't cause cyberbullying. But these digital technology platforms do make it easier. Half of all young people ages fourteen to twenty-four have experienced digitally abusive behavior.[18]

As cyberbullying has seeped into the national consciousness, many states have begun passing laws that target bullying on the Internet and social networks. Schools have begun new education programs for students and faculty, and millions of parents have become more aware and involved. At Common Sense Media, we work with major media and tech companies—from Google and Facebook to MTV, Nickelodeon, and Disney, to name a few—to promote anti-cyberbullying campaigns and to develop concrete methods to prevent its occurrence. This is no longer an issue that is in the shadows.

My fourteen-year-old daughter does not have a Facebook page, as of this writing, largely because of some mean behavior and catty remarks she has personally experienced, online and offline, among girls in her peer group. She's very aware of cyberbullying issues and how the social life of some of her classmates has changed because of online experiences. Other parents have told me how their kids have been hurt or made to feel profoundly stressed and insecure through online interactions with peers and classmates. I know of cases in which friends have sent their kids away for significant periods of time to special schools or camps that strictly ban Facebook and cell phones. I also know several families who have elected to have their children change schools because of mean social behaviors on online platforms.

Let's be clear: I'm not blaming Facebook or cell phone companies for the cruel, abusive, or creepy behavior of some users. That said, social network companies need to acknowledge that they have a responsibility to help change these behaviors and establish and codify clear, ethical social norms in the new world they're bringing into being. Whether you're a parent, a teacher, or a tech industry leader, we all have our work cut out for us.

Digital Depression

In early 2011, the American Academy of Pediatrics (AAP) warned that teens who use social network sites and compare their profiles to those of friends and classmates are more vulnerable to anxiety and what the AAP calls "Facebook depression." Depression has also been linked to digital gaming. Ever since I watched my son Kirk and his pals become fixated on games like World of Warcraft and FIFA Soccer, I've wondered whether too much game playing could have an impact on their mental health. Two studies published in recent months suggest that there is, indeed, a link. One study, published in 2011 in the medical journal *Pediatrics,* traced the behavior of about three thousand kids in Singapore in grades three to eight, over a two-year period. The researchers found that children who were generally more impulsive and less comfortable with other kids spent considerably more time playing video games. At the end of the two years, these heavy gamers, who played for an average of thirty-one hours a week, were found to suffer more from anxiety, social fears, and depression. They were also more likely to see their school performance decline and have less positive relationships with their parents.[19]

A second study, published in the *Archives of Pediatric and Adolescent Medicine,* studied more than a thousand Chinese teenagers between the ages of thirteen and eighteen. The results were remarkably similar. Teens who used the Internet excessively were more than twice as likely to feel depressed nine months later than those teens who used it in normal amounts, and the majority of the depressed teens spent most of their Internet time playing video games.[20]

These studies both came from Asian countries, where issues related to video game addiction and related mental health problems are more openly addressed. Indeed, in Korea, there are now special programs and camps to treat kids who are addicted to video games. Studies in the United States bolster these findings. Research by Douglas Gentile, a professor of psychology at Iowa State, found that kids who are more impulsive and less socially adept are more likely to retreat into the virtual worlds of gaming. The more their gaming increases, the more their grades drop, and the more they become estranged from their parents. After two years, these heavy gamers are more likely to suffer from depression and deep-seated social anxiety. In a sense, what researchers refer to as "pathological gaming" fosters a spiral of alienation and isolation in vulnerable teens. We cannot say for certain whether these kids suffered only because they were heavy gamers, but there appears to be a strong association.

At Common Sense Media, we've worked to publicize the demonstrable public health risks associated with video games and to develop laws regulating the sale of ultraviolent and sexually violent video games to minors. Some of those laws were recently struck down on First Amendment grounds by the industry-friendly U.S. Supreme Court. Our work on video games, however, has made it clear that the games can have significant consequences for heavy users, especially teen boys. Some of the violent content is simply disgusting; I've had to view a lot of it in my job at Common Sense. To me, it resembles violent pornography. The addictive nature of many of the most violent games also seems crystal clear to a number of public health experts. Whether you choose to believe the link between heavy video game use and psychological depression, there can be no doubt that many kids retreat into the world of video games far too often, for unhealthy periods of time.

The issue of violent video games won't go away, and the industry needs to be held accountable. Video game companies are highly unlikely to rein themselves in voluntarily. We are talking big bucks here. In 2010, more than $25 billion was spent on the games industry, and the video game industry today is much bigger, in financial terms, than the movie industry. The good news is that educators and talented developers are finding creative new ways to turn games into exciting educational content. At Common Sense Media, we're on the forefront of facilitating this educational progress, and we're producing our own educational interactive games. But the bad news is that some developers continue to include extremely objectionable content in their games. In doing so, they expose millions of kids daily to inappropriate messages and images that, in certain cases, can lead to addiction and depression. As parents and educators, we should do everything in our power to encourage and expand the positive, educational potential of video games while being vigilant and outspoken about limiting damage to our kids. That's our job as parents and teachers.

The Good News About Technology and Relationships

I've offered this critique of the new 24/7 digital media world because I believe it's incredibly important for parents, educators, and young people to wake up to its negative trends. These issues cut to the core of our children's social, emotional, and cognitive development. Because the digital revolution has spread with such extraordinary velocity and impact, many of us are just beginning to appreciate what it means for our families, our kids, and our society's future.

That said, I believe it's very important to take a balanced approach to these shifts in media and technology. That's why, at Common Sense Media, we emphasize the possibilities as much as the dangers. We don't cry wolf, and we certainly don't view the new technology platforms as monolithic or inherently bad or good. Since the genie is out of the bottle, it's important to accept that reality and make the best of the situation wherever possible.

I'm sure that the folks at Facebook and other social networks may think I don't call out all the positives enough. They might point to a 2010 study jointly conducted by the Pew Research Center and the University of Pennsylvania Annenberg School of Communications that indicated that there were positive social benefits for adults who used Facebook and other social networks. These Facebook users, the research showed, felt they could trust people, friends, and colleagues on the social network and were more politically active because of their Facebook connections. The site also helped them retain high school friendships and revive dormant relationships.[21]

In my experience, those positives are indeed true for adults, and I've also heard from parents and teachers who feel that technology platforms like social networks and instant messaging can help bring shy children out of their shell in important ways. I'm aware, too, that, according to new research from the University of Maryland, spending time on Facebook and other social media can help kids in school build helpful bonds with other students. I personally believe that when Facebook and other social networks are used responsibly, they can bring many positive benefits to kids' friendships and social relationships. Many young people derive social benefits and personal satisfaction from using social media to keep in touch with friends, share information, and simply hang out like normal teenagers.

It's also true, however, that adults are far more likely than kids to use Facebook and other social networks responsibly and productively. The bottom line, for parents and teachers alike, is that we have to become more aware and engaged with our kids' media and technology lives. Period. The more we can mentor and guide our children, the better they'll handle these new platforms. Because our actions are just as important as our words, we must model responsible technology use and behavior for our children in our own lives.[22]

But involvement from parents and teachers simply isn't enough. We deeply need an open and ongoing national discussion about the pros and cons of digital media behavior and its effects on kids in every home and school across the country. These issues are so new that the average person is just beginning to wake up to their impact. Fortunately, the dialogue is finally beginning. To promote it, we should require the media and technology industries to support a national public awareness campaign promoting positive and responsible uses of cell phones, video games, social networks, and other digital platforms. And we should fund major new research studies on the impact of digital media on young people's social and emotional development.

During the past three years, Common Sense Media has created a state-of-the-art K–12 curriculum focused on "Digital Literacy and Citizenship" that is now used in more than 25,000 schools across the United States. The curriculum is designed to give young people critical thinking skills and digital "rules of the road"—a simple, concise list of behaviors that promote the safe, ethical, and responsible use of media and technology across all digital platforms. We all need to know basic social etiquette—covering everything from conversation and ethics to cyber-bullying and sexting—on digital platforms, and we need to codify these norms for kids and adults.

Following the advice of leading child development experts, we must also emphasize the need for regular time-outs and downtime from our devices. And we clearly need much more scientific and psychological research to more fully identify both the positive and negative impacts of technology on our brains and psyches. In the end, however, in this almost limitless new world of digital devices and social media, it's up to each of us, individually and collectively, to make sure that our kids, not just the tech companies, are the biggest winners.

Chapter Two

Attention and Addiction Issues: Your Child's Brain on Computers

We shape our tools, and thereafter our tools shape us.
—Marshall McLuhan, media commentator

Hanging out with perpetually wired teenagers these days can be a pretty jarring experience for any adult. The average American teen today seems to be doing a hundred things at once—watching videos on YouTube, Facebooking, and texting with their friends—their brains bouncing from one activity to another, often in a matter of seconds. Maybe I've been teaching at Stanford for too long, but you can't tell me that this constant digital distraction doesn't have an impact on some of my students' ability to focus on a particular subject, to get their homework done well, and to write clear and coherent papers. I now get term papers that seem more disjointed than a few years ago and see students using Internet slang or text-message misspellings in their work.

You don't need to be a neuroscientist to observe these changes, in both kids and adults. Indeed, scientists and researchers confirm that the Internet may actually be changing how our brains work. Some researchers take images of the brain over time. Others make inferences about what is happening in the brain based on what people think or how they behave. In that light, I use the terms "brain" and "mind" interchangeably in this chapter.

Online behavior has neurological consequences, especially in children and teens whose brains are still developing. In fact, leading scientific researchers believe that brain development changes linked to media are occurring in our youngest children. According to a study led by Dimitri Christakis of the University of Washington's School of Medicine, every hour of television that kids watched each day from age one through three increased their risk of attention problems at age seven by nearly 10 percent.[1]

In his recent book, *The Shallows: What the Internet Is Doing to Our Brains,* author Nicholas Carr asked the basic question "Is Google making us stupid?"[2] Analyzing everything from neuroscience to increasing changes in our ability to concentrate, write, and reflect, Carr concluded that our new world of digital immersion has changed everything from logical thought processes and work habits to our capacity for linear thinking. As he puts it, "Calm, focused, undistracted, the linear mind is being pushed aside by a new kind of mind that wants and needs to take in and dole out information in short, disjointed, often overlapping bursts—the faster, the better."[3]

Previously, many doctors and scientists assumed that brain circuitry was malleable only in childhood and that it became fixed and hardwired once people reached adulthood. Recent neurological studies, however, reveal that adult brains have much more "plasticity" and are far more changeable than previously recognized. Researchers have observed these changes in how taxi drivers experience spatial representation and the growth of the brains of violinists. In short, our brains are a work in progress, and the digital revolution has had an enormous impact, most especially on the brain structure and chemistry of young kids and teens.[4]

New York Times reporter Matt Richtel told me recently that digital devices are tapping into the "deepest, most primitive neurological impulses that we have." The constant bombardment of stimuli from text messages and Facebook pings are actively stimulating the impulse-driven section of young people's lower brains. At the same time, the prefrontal cortex—the center of judgment, rational planning, and orderly thinking—doesn't mature until approximately age twenty-three. It's the last part of the brain to fully develop. Researchers who explore this field, Richtel says, worry that young people's brains, in particular, are in a relatively continuous state of civil war between the weak, advanced frontal lobe functions (order, logic, and planning) and the more primitive, impulse-driven instincts of the lower brain area. Not surprisingly, fifteen-year-olds, who receive an average of nearly thirty-five hundred text messages per month, may be developing the impulse, "fast-twitch" portions of their brains far more than the logic- and planning-focused frontal portions.[5]

Leading researchers like Paul Atchley, a professor at the University of Kansas who studies teenagers' compulsive use of mobile phones, believe that young people's heavy use of "interruption technologies" can impede deep thinking and cause them increased social and emotional anxiety.[6] Moreover, TV and newspaper media content is being increasingly chopped up to fit the shorter attention spans of young consumers who are becoming habituated to the fast, distracting pace of digital media. Experts like Dimitri Christakis, while careful to emphasize that ADHD has an important genetic component as well, believe that there needs to be far more study of the impact of media and technology on attention problems and brain development overall.[7]

The Myth of Multitasking

In 2009, Stanford communications professor Cliff Nass and his colleagues conducted a pioneering research study that demonstrated that heavy multitaskers were actually more prone to distractions and irrelevant information and performed worse than others on tests designed to measure their ability to focus clearly and switch successfully between tasks.[8] The image of the modern wired techie, successfully juggling information and simultaneously processing multiple streams of data, is essentially a total myth.

Young people have always been drawn to distractions and found ways to waste time. My own teenage years were no exception, and I found many imaginative ways to avoid schoolwork and other responsibilities. But today's ever-increasing stimuli from the Internet and cell phones present unique challenges to kids' ability to learn and concentrate in school. And even though some teachers and parents are concerned about the digital onslaught, most schools around the country are becoming increasingly technology focused and encourage the use of computers and other digital devices at home. Of course, we need to take advantage of their educational and human development potential, and we actively support the appropriate use of technology to further twenty-first-century learning. That said, we also see a need for healthy balance and for schools to choose the appropriate times and places for technology use.

The impact of media multitasking on students' homework and related academic performance represents an important issue for educators to consider. Since students increasingly rely on computers and other digital devices as part of their course of study, schools must reinforce clear rules about the proper, healthy use of digital media in both homework and research. Clearly, watching a five-minute video on YouTube should never substitute for reading the full text of a Shakespeare play. In short, schools at all levels need to explicitly recognize the increasing digital distractions that many young people face and help prevent students from getting lost between the competing demands of virtual reality and their important academic responsibilities.

Diminishing Downtime

Growing scientific research also underscores the critical importance of "media time-outs" in our lives, particularly for kids and teens who have developing brains. Mental downtime is another casualty of our connected lives. All of us, kids and adults alike, have a fundamental need for regular breaks from the Ping Pong–like distractions of digital stimuli.

Many of us know the simple pleasures of going to a vacation spot where cell phones and e-mails don't work and all laptops and iPads are left behind. It can be so calming and peaceful when we fully unplug from our devices. Our brains relax. We sleep better. We escape the constant pinging of our cell phones and Internet notifications. Our ideas and imaginations begin to flow as we experience true, uninterrupted downtime from our digital lives.

For children and teens, that kind of downtime is really essential. Constant digital stimulation not only affects young people's ability to focus and pay attention, but it can also affect their memory development. I'm not a mind and brain scientist, and the research on digital media and memory is in its early stages, but here is a thumbnail sketch, based on what I've learned from leading experts in the field. Our basic depth of intelligence depends on our ability to transfer information from our working memory to our long-term memory, then to use that information conceptually. There's a bit of a bottleneck in the system, because working memory has a much smaller capacity than long-term memory, and the transfer takes time. When the information load in our working memory is too large and exceeds our brain's capacity to store and process it, that information is lost. This "memory loss" occurs when our brains are overly distracted and overtaxed. The Internet, smartphones, and other digital devices can be the source of exactly this type of information overload. And unfortunately, human memory doesn't function like a hard drive that absorbs and stores data in fixed locations and retrieves it as needed.

Too much hypertext and multimedia content, supposedly a boon to learning, is often related to limited attention span, lower comprehension, and less focus. It can also be associated with information/cognitive overload, and diminished long-term memory. It's true that careful combinations of audio and visual content can, if structured appropriately, enhance learning skills, but the Internet and most Web content wasn't built with that goal in mind. Like most digital media, they're designed for interruption. And the interruptive process scatters thoughts, taxes mental resources, and can ultimately impair long-term memory. It may also undermine deep creative thinking, inductive analysis, and critical thinking skills.

Studies of how students use research websites, for example, show large amounts of skimming as they bounce impatiently from article to article. Some brain functions, like fast problem solving and adept data juggling, can be enhanced by such activities, and this mental nimbleness shouldn't be underestimated. But the interruptive process can also affect our capacities for imagination, reflection, and concentration—and, oh yes, our ability to remember things. In kids, whose brains are far less developed, the impacts can be significantly magnified. So there you have it—my simple-minded, nonscientific explanation of your child's brain on computers.[9]

Sleep is another important function that can be disrupted by too much digital stimulation. If you think about it, this isn't particularly surprising, since quality sleep is basically a form of downtime. And as all parents know, or should know, sleep is a crucial aspect of a child's healthy social, emotional, and physical development. Recent research suggests that digital devices and technology can interfere with healthy sleep patterns in a couple of ways. First, a lot of older kids now take their cell phones, gaming devices, and laptops into bed with them at night. Many text each other late when they should be sleeping, arousing their brains while waiting for friends to text them back. Teens, in fact, send more than a third of their texts after lights are out. A lot of other kids play digital games before bed, a habit that can also be disruptive to sleep. Rapidly sequenced video games and popular apps like Angry Birds stimulate the brain, exactly what sleep experts advise against at bedtime. Instead, they recommend calming, relaxed activities, which is one reason why reading to kids is always so highly recommended. So, parents, take note: sleep is essential to mental downtime, and it can easily be compromised by too much digital media.

Driven to Distraction

In 2010, journalist Matt Richtel won a Pulitzer Prize for a series of *New York Times* articles he wrote cataloging the growing dangers and increasing collisions between two major technological advances of the twentieth

41

and twenty-first centuries: driving and media multitasking. His series "Driven to Distraction" helped spawn a series of legislative efforts in states across the country to ban the use of cell phones and texting while driving and requiring drivers to use hands-free headsets. Growing concerns about the dangers of distracted driving, especially among teenagers, also forced the cell phone and automobile industries, which had previously downplayed the problem, to support new limits and public awareness campaigns about the risks of this increasingly common practice.[10] Unfortunately, we've all seen people texting or BlackBerrying while driving, oblivious to the deadly dangers resulting from this lack of focus, and statistics on teen accidents and deaths related to texting and driving are especially troubling.

Researchers believe these dangers are related to the way the brain takes in information. Essentially, humans can't effectively process two streams of information at once. If you don't believe the research, try this experiment: stand at a party or in a crowded room and have a conversation with the person in front of you. Listen to what they're saying. Then also try to listen to what the person behind you is saying. You might be able to hear a name or something very simple, but you won't be able to process both streams of information simultaneously or remember much of either. Now try it with three conversations at once—it's impossible. While you're at it, ask your perpetually wired teenager to give this experiment a try. Similarly, if you're engaged in a phone conversation or texting, even if your hands are on the wheel, you're processing a stream of information that's completely separate from the information stream that your brain needs to process so you can drive safely. People often get away with it because driving can be a fairly routine experience, but you're lucky if your distractedness doesn't cause an accident.

Research suggests that this dangerously split focus occurs even during hands-free phone conversations. Even though your hands generally stay on the wheel where they belong, you're still overloading your brain with two information streams at the same time. Your functioning is impaired. If a car swerves into your lane or stops suddenly or, God forbid, a child walks in front of your car unexpectedly while you're on the phone, you lose key milliseconds to make critical decisions and necessary adjustments to avoid an accident. That's why distracted driving is so very dangerous. Yet for many drivers, both teens and adults, cell phones and BlackBerrys are hard to put down or turn off despite the hazards. Why? I believe it's because these devices, and our use of them, have led to compulsive behavior and in some cases have become addictive.

Addiction to Digital Devices

Stephanie Brown, a widely respected psychologist and director of the Addictions Institute in Menlo Park, California, says she's seeing more and more families in her practice where both the kids and parents can't tear themselves away from their digital devices. With kids, she's encountering increasing problems with electronic gaming. As she puts it,

> Addictions happen when people are trying to control their emotional state. You find something that makes you feel better and then you want more of it, but then there is emptiness in the payoff. We're seeing that, overnight, the happy little soccer player becomes the addicted gamer on World of Warcraft.[11]

One fifteen-year-old boy I know—an introvert I'll call Jack—is obsessed with video games. He plays about four hours daily after school and sometimes double that on weekends—switching between Call of Duty, the popular violent game where you can stalk and kill terrorists and other bad guys, and World of Warcraft, the phenomenally successful multiplayer online game. Jack says it's a way to separate himself from the stress of his daily life and his nagging parents. Most afternoons, he just goes to his room, closes his door, and escapes into his private world of fantasy games. He sometimes wishes that his parents would intervene and make him quit playing and study more, but he doesn't blame the games; instead, he acknowledges there's some emptiness in his life, and the buzz and excitement of digital games helps fill the void.

Digital dependency is controversial, and not all experts and psychologists agree with the addiction metaphor. Stanford communications professor Byron Reeves argues that "the term addiction [when used with gaming] can cause trouble. Does it mean playing too long? What is too long?" Professor Reeves believes that there can be a number of positive effects from extended game play; he cites one study showing that teens who play multiplayer games often have more friends in their social life and a lower BMI (Body Mass Index).[12] He has also cofounded a new Silicon Valley company, Seriosity, to develop online games. Still, Reeves acknowledges that some gamers play too much.

David Sheff, the author of the best-selling memoir *Beautiful Boy: A Father's Journey Through His Son's Addiction,* scoffs at such distinctions when it comes to video games and other digital media. Sheff is convinced that the addiction model applies to video games and other digital content, and he notes that there are rehablike programs in Korea that treat video game addicts, mostly teenagers.[13] He also argues that, in his experience, video games are often used like drugs and alcohol to block depressive feelings. As MIT's Sherry Turkle points out, vulnerable teens often use digital devices to keep feelings at a distance and hide behind a deliberate outward appearance of nonchalance.[14] Addiction, Sheff explains, is indicated by measured neurological changes in the brain and sometimes related physiological and psychological effects, and scientists have seen clear neurological changes from heavy video game use. Unlike gaming, he believes, digital stimuli like repeated texting, IMing, or Facebooking may be more psychologically than physically addicting, but they still have highly addictive qualities. Dimitri Christakis, the pediatric brain researcher, agrees with Sheff: "I definitely believe digital media use is addictive," he says. "Like other addictions, it's a combination of genetic predisposition, coupled with exposure to those behaviors."[15]

There's something very serious at play here. We all know teens and adults whose devices are almost like security blankets. Turkle and other researchers talk about teens who use their phones so constantly that it eliminates the privacy and solitude required for true intimacy as well as the space that's necessary for self-reflection. Experts also observe that this constant connectedness can be associated with increased feelings of anxiety as well as the stress of always being "on call," especially among young people who are tethered to their devices and Facebook profiles.[16] For some heavy users, digital media can get in the way of sleeping, exercising, socializing, and even showering.

If you agree, as I do, that video games, Facebook, smartphones, and other digital media can be truly addictive, and at the very least compulsive, the question becomes what to do about it. Going cold turkey isn't much of an option. David Sheff notes that with drugs or alcohol, the addiction is "latent," so the best solution in those cases is not to prime the pump and to abstain completely. Media addiction, however, he believes, is more like food addiction. Even foodaholics have to eat, but the key is to do so in moderation while dealing with dependency issues.[17] With digital media, it's all about balance and moderation. That sounds pretty sensible to me.

As parents, we need to model this balanced approach to digital media use, because our kids are watching and following our example. We all need to take regular time-outs from technology, and experts recommend that we should enjoy significant stretches of time without interruptions or the distractions of digital devices. Taking time to unplug is clearly important for mental health and for minimizing our compulsive and addictive tendencies. Most of all, it will undoubtedly improve the quality of our human relationships, especially with family and friends.

Chapter Three

The Loss of Privacy: Why Your Child Is at Risk

People have really gotten comfortable not only sharing more information and different kinds, but more openly and with more people. That social norm is something that has evolved over time.[1]

—Mark Zuckerberg, Facebook CEO

Imagine the following true story happening to your son or daughter. A thirteen-year-old girl took a nude picture of herself with her cell phone and sent it to her eighth-grade boyfriend. After they broke up, he sent the picture to another girl in the class, who labeled the image "Ho Alert!" and texted it to every person on her contact list. Then those teens forwarded the picture to their friends; in a matter of hours, hundreds of the girl's schoolmates and maybe thousands of other people had seen it. For months afterward, the young girl in the photograph was viciously taunted, online and offline; struggling with depression, she had to change schools twice. Her ex-boyfriend was handcuffed, taken to jail, and charged with disseminating child pornography, a felony offense. Two naïve, vulnerable middle schoolers

46

were devastated by the modern-day horrors of unerasable, irrevocable digital life.[2]

When I first heard this story, my heart went out to the parents and kids involved, and I wondered how I would handle a situation like that. But it also made me think about an enormous society-transforming issue that lies at the heart of this tragic story: privacy, or more specifically, the increasing *absence* of privacy in a viral, Web-obsessed culture, where there is no "eraser" button.

I started this chapter with a quote from Facebook CEO Mark Zuckerberg for a reason. Today, it's difficult to have a meaningful discussion about increasing privacy concerns and their impact on kids and families without discussing Facebook. Like it or not, its platform, business model, and policies have helped give rise to many of the most serious issues related to privacy for kids and consumers. Zuckerberg's assertion that the "social norm . . . has evolved" reveals much to me about the mind-set of Facebook and other tech companies. In the past few years, they have rather summarily called our long-held, fundamental right to personal privacy into question, with enormous implications for everyone, especially vulnerable young people.

To me, Zuckerberg's quote, as well as Facebook's ever-shifting privacy policies, speak to a larger cultural issue driven by a largely libertarian, Silicon Valley approach to life that seems to value data over human beings. It's like these companies are saying, "Our search for data and our aggregation of your personal information is all important, so just figure out a way to deal with the social and emotional consequences as your privacy disappears." The lack of serious reflection—you could call it a dismissive attitude—about the critically important norms of privacy is hardly Mark Zuckerberg's fault alone, even if he happens to be the poster child for this point of view.

When CNBC asked Eric Schmidt, executive chairman and former CEO of the search giant Google, a similar question about privacy concerns, he opined: "If you have something that you don't want anyone to know, maybe you shouldn't be doing it in the first place."[3] In a subsequent interview with the *Wall Street Journal*, Schmidt predicted that in the future there would be no need to worry about privacy because young people would be automatically entitled to change their names to escape their online pasts.[4] Maybe Schmidt was just kidding, but online privacy settings aren't always clear, so people easily make mistakes. That's especially true for kids who don't always have great judgment and are often prone to experimentation. Young people, and many adults, now routinely post and share private, personal information and opinions on platforms like Facebook and Twitter without fully considering the potential consequences. The impulse-enabling nature of social media platforms, coupled with the vulnerable and inexperienced social and emotional development of many young people, can be combustible. Millions of kids say and do things that they later regret, and because of the permanence and persistence of the Internet and digital media—the lack of an "eraser" button—the embarrassment and damage can last forever. The information and photos can be passed on and stored by many other websites, with far-reaching consequences.

Common Sense Media has conducted a couple of major national polls of kids' and parents' attitudes toward privacy in the last two years, and the results speak volumes about this problem. For example, 39 percent (two out of five) of all American teens, ages thirteen through seventeen, *admit* that they have personally posted something online that they've later regretted, and 28 percent of all teens admit that they have shared personal information about themselves online that they would not have shared in public. In addition, 79 percent of all American teens (four out of five) think their friends share too much personal information online, and 58 percent of American teens (three out of five) fear that sharing too much online could keep them from getting into college or getting a job in the future.

Adults who were polled on this topic tend to be a bit more discreet, perhaps due to their age and more mature judgment, but 20 percent of American adults polled in 2010 *admit* that they've personally posted something online that they've later regretted.[5] And virtually every parent and teacher I know worries about their children or teens making this kind of mistake and the potential consequences. So what are we to think when respected tech leaders say that the solution to this problem is for people to just change their names?

I should add that I have met with Eric Schmidt several times over the past few years. I like him a lot personally, and I know that he's a loving dad and an excellent business executive. Common Sense Media has had several very meaningful partnerships with Google related to kids and education, and Schmidt and his colleagues care a lot about education and the broader public interest. I have also had conversations with the senior executives at Facebook. I recognize that these tech leaders have many good personal qualities, and Mark Zuckerberg has personally donated $100 million to Newark, New Jersey's public schools. These are clearly not evil people. That said, their statements are highly revealing of their companies' attitudes toward your and my privacy and the extraordinary changes that have occurred in recent years. These attitudes help explain why our society's deep commitment to privacy has been so rapidly eviscerated, while Silicon Valley tech giants focus on aggregating data, personal information, and profit and largely ignore the consequences for children and families.

Lest you think that it's only parents, children's advocates, and consumer organizations who are decrying the invasions of personal privacy wrought by technology companies in their all-encompassing pursuit of data and profit, consider the reasoning of high-tech pioneer Jaron Lanier. One of the leading visionaries in the field, he has been one of the most important voices criticizing Facebook and other social networks. These companies get most of their profits from advertisers, whose goal is to get as much information about consumers as possible. Advertisers are the paying customers of a social network or search engine, and the raw material that advertisers want is the personal data and information of users. As Lanier sees it, this basic business model of social networks essentially dictates that they have little interest in protecting consumers' privacy. In addition, Lanier and other leading tech thinkers have also spoken out against Google and geolocation services like Foursquare and Loopt, which track users' whereabouts. Lanier has compared them to "privatized spy agencies," which accumulate your personal information without giving you, or your kids, an easy way to opt out.[6] As Facebook's record-setting IPO occurs, these enormously profound societal issues will only become more important and should become the subject of a major national debate.

Privacy: A Basic Framework

So why does privacy matter so much, particularly for children and teens? In my opinion, the privacy debate can be separated into two essential and related parts.

First is what we at Common Sense refer to as the "self-revealing before self-reflecting" problem. Young people, and too many adults, now routinely post and share private, personal information and opinions on platforms like Facebook and Twitter without fully considering the potential consequences, which can be catastrophic.

Second, the basic business models and corporate strategies of many of the world's leading technology giants are focused on tracking and aggregating personal data and information from consumers. They monitor what you click on and track your preferences. A primary point is to use or sell this personal data for commercial gain, frequently to advertisers or other marketers. Another point is to provide more personalized offerings tailored to your interests. As such, these large companies have a vested interest in convincing consumers to share as much personal information as possible so that they can collect it and put it to commercial use. Put simply, your personal data and information is the source of much of their profit. For example, Facebook made $3.2 billion in advertising revenue in 2011, 85 percent of its total revenue, and this is the lead up to the biggest IPO in history. And Google took in an estimated $36.5 billion in advertising revenue in 2011. Needless to say, that's not chicken feed!

As a result, the tech industry has little interest in protecting your or my privacy. Indeed, it is precisely the opposite. Leading tech companies have a clear economic motive for intruding upon our privacy and obtaining as much data and personal information as they can. It's about profit, and it allows them to serve you up more targeted advertising. Sure, corporate privacy policies do exist, but they are often seventy pages long, completely confusing, full of legalistic jargon, and buried at the bottom of an app or Web page you're unlikely to read. Even if you read them, most policies don't really offer much protection. They're more accurately "information use policies" than "privacy policies."

Taken together, these twin pillars of the broader privacy framework have led to a fundamental change in society's treatment of privacy and the personal lives of millions. This change has occurred virtually overnight, in the span of a few short years, with little public awareness or public leadership and virtually no meaningful public debate.

This is not a trivial issue. Privacy has long been held to be a basic right of citizens in our society. I have taught constitutional law and courses on civil rights and civil liberties to undergrads at Stanford for the past twenty-five years. As my students and many American adults know, or should know, "privacy" has been held to be a "fundamental right" by the U.S. Supreme Court. In fact, *Roe v. Wade,* the famous 1974 abortion decision, was premised on the recognition by all the Supreme Court Justices that privacy is a fundamental right under the Fourteenth Amendment to the U.S. Constitution. In all subsequent abortion cases, no Justice—and indeed no serious advocate, irrespective of their position on abortion— has ever argued that privacy is not a fundamental right of all persons in the United States. These cases have, instead, focused on balancing a woman's fundamental right to privacy versus the perceived rights of fetuses, as well as related arguments about when "life" begins. Indeed, some states, including California, also include privacy as an explicitly recognized and fundamental right in their constitutions.

The point of this brief legal tutorial is merely to underscore the importance of privacy as a fundamental right in American history and culture. We recognize very few "fundamental rights" in our society, so the fact that our legal and constitutional system enshrines privacy in this manner should not be forgotten in the broader discussion about technology and kids. The last time I checked, large corporate interests aren't allowed to trample on widely recognized fundamental rights because their founders have invented some new, profitable privacy-busting product. Yet that is exactly what has happened to privacy rights over the past few years.

Most of our elected leaders and citizens have been largely passive and mute as this enormous social change has been taking hold. Many government officials have essentially abdicated their leadership responsibilities when it comes to privacy and frequently accept large campaign contributions from the tech industry. The last national children's privacy law was passed in 1998, aeons ago in Internet time. Since then, consumers and kids have largely been left to the whims of the marketplace. The good news, however, is that the privacy debate is finally beginning to take hold in the United States and across the globe, and none too soon. The bad news is that we've already experienced many negative consequences.

Self-Revealing Without Self-Reflecting

A host of recent stories involving sexting, cyberbullying, and other tragic but typical teen behaviors make all too real the consequences of this lack of respect for our fundamental right to personal privacy.

Sexting, for example, poses significant privacy issues for today's teens and young adults. In fact, 71 percent of young adults consider sexting to be a serious problem among people their age.[7] Not only do young people forget to self-reflect before they self-reveal, but many recipients of sexting messages are also mindless, if not downright cruel, when it comes to sharing such photos. When eighth-graders can distribute a naked photo of a female classmate online to hundreds of other students, accompanied by insulting messages about the girl,[8] it is easy to see the enormous consequences of such privacy violations.

It's almost too obvious to bear repeating that young people frequently make mistakes; indeed, they often reveal too much of themselves before they fully consider or understand the consequences. It's called being a teenager. As child psychologists increasingly make clear, however, the anonymity of the Web and the impersonal nature of digital devices encourage impulsivity and people's darker sides.

Another related example is the practice of "Facebook stalking," which occurs when users search Facebook to deeply investigate other people's profiles and information. Many younger Facebook users know that people will "stalk" one another, so it may not feel as threatening as cyberbullying, but it can also bring out the more mean-spirited side of kids and teens when they critique and gossip about the profiles of other users. Moreover, this common practice can be addictive and a huge waste of time. It often comes up in conversations with teens; many feel it violates whatever sense of privacy they have and causes real anxiety. My older daughter admits that it's very common to look at other people's walls and conversations on Facebook without their knowledge. But she calls this practice "highly creepy," feels uncomfortable about it, and compares it to listening in on people's phone calls. This is also a practice that's being automated by background check services, which employers and others are now using as they evaluate people for various roles.

Young people also face another common and painful form of digital drama: online impersonation and "hacking." This occurs when someone gets hold of your Facebook or MySpace profile, pretends to be you, changes the layout or content, or sends messages in your name. This malicious behavior can be devastating, and there's virtually no recourse. If you tamper with regular snail mail via the post office, it's a crime, but generally, when your Facebook page is hacked, it's your problem to solve. As the parent of a teenager who has been "hacked," I can assure you that it's no laughing matter.

Though photo "tagging" is not considered a form of digital abuse, it can also have damaging consequences. On Facebook, "tagging" is a way for you to publicly identify your friends in photos. If you are tagged, not only will you see your name beneath your friend's photo, but you may also find a copy of the image on your profile for others to see. This can be fun if you are tagged in flattering photos from group outings or in photos that are inside jokes. But depending on your privacy settings, it could also mean that your life is on full display—to college admissions counselors or potential employers, for example—with a permanent digital record, without your okay and with no control over where the photos end up permanently. For example, if a teen is at a party and somewhat inebriated or doing something silly or embarrassing, some random person can snap a photo with his phone, post it on the Internet, and then tag the names of everyone in the picture. Needless to say, there can often be major consequences. Even teens who are diligent about untagging themselves often fail to realize, or care about, the fact that those pictures still exist online, regardless of whether their names are listed beneath them.

Recently, under pressure, Facebook changed its policy so that users can choose to approve tagged pictures before they're posted, but you still have to go to Privacy Settings and "opt in" to that feature. It's not the default setting; protecting your privacy is not Facebook's business. The company's basic mantra and business practice is always to encourage as much "sharing" as possible. When there's widespread resistance from users, the company retreats, but only temporarily; it soon makes other attempts to encourage users to share more data.

In the summer of 2011, under competitive pressure from the launch of Google Plus, which gave social network users a bit more control over personal information, Facebook once again altered certain aspects of its privacy policies, making its service more similar to that of Google Plus. It appeared to be a positive step for privacy, but it didn't last long. A few months later, Facebook introduced new features like "Timeline" and "Open Graph," which expose even more personal information about your online activity in a manner that Mark Zuckerberg termed "frictionless sharing." The idea behind "frictionless sharing" is that Facebook users will no longer have to rely on the "Like" button to flag something that interests them. Instead, Facebook apps can automatically share what you've recently checked out online: the music you have listened to, the recipes you want to cook, the articles that you have read, and more.

Zuckerberg described Timeline as an opportunity to "curate" the stories that express your online self. In some ways, he's right. Users will have all of seven days to select what they want to share on their Timeline before it's published. They'll get to sift through years of data and create a visual autobiography of how they've evolved over the years. At least that's how Facebook hopes we'll see it. But that's not my personal take on the new products, nor is it the assessment of other thoughtful analysts. The *New York Times* headlined its analysis of Timeline: "Your Life on Facebook in Total Recall." As Harvard law professor and Internet expert Jonathan Zittrain noted in the *Times* article, "There's no act too small to record on your permanent record. All of the mouse droppings that appear as we migrate around the Web will be saved."[9] To me, that sure sounds very troubling from a personal privacy perspective, especially where young and often emotionally careless teenagers are concerned. Who wants their total life to be on display?

Timeline and Open Graph also make it far more difficult for users to keep control over their self-presentations. One of a number of serious privacy concerns about Timeline is that it exposes information that people rarely looked at or cared about before. Timeline makes it much easier for people to peruse your long-forgotten posts and pictures and judge what you acted like in the past.[10] The tech site ZDNet bluntly called these new features "a stalker's paradise." Others agreed that they could be "a treat for profile stalkers" and warned that Facebook users had little control over how their personal information could be shared.[11] Indeed, Facebook often tries to put users' data to profitable commercial use via its advertisers. That's the underlying business rationale for all its lofty claims of "frictionless sharing."

When my Common Sense colleagues and I discuss all these issues with young people who use Facebook, they admit that these matters are serious concerns, but they don't know what they can do about them. Even kids who try to use the strictest privacy settings say that Facebook often changes the policy at will and that it's almost impossible to control what happens. A number of teens with whom I've spoken seem almost resigned to living in a stressful, nonprivate reality, and that infuriates me. We as a society should not accept this reality and should demand that it change.

Why is the privacy of millions of kids and many adults put at risk with so little public discussion and outcry? I simply do not buy Mark Zuckerberg's comments about "changing social norms," or the frequent assertion by tech industry leaders that young people today don't care about their personal privacy. I think they do care, very much, about their privacy, feelings, and intimate relationships. They just don't know what life was like before Facebook, what privacy protections they're *entitled* to, and where to turn for answers. Many of the adults on whom they would normally rely for guidance don't understand Facebook's privacy policy either—in 2010, it was longer than that of all other social networks as well as the U.S. Constitution, without amendments—and they don't understand what tools they can use for their protection. Essentially, it's the blind leading the blind.

When large tech companies argue that they get to use your private information for their own profit, it's important to consider the consequences. Perhaps you didn't reflect carefully before posting a photo. Perhaps someone posed as you, or a "friend" posted something about you without your permission. It's not just that a drunken image of you at a party or a post that calls you a "slut" could be seen by thousands of "friends," college counselors, and future employers. Even more important, this digital record may be out there permanently and largely out of your control.

Adolescent psychologists such as Erik Erikson have always talked about the importance of the teen years being a time for identity exploration and experimentation. This is a normal and healthy part of growing up, even if it drives some parents crazy. But this critically important developmental phase is dramatically twisted when identity experimentation, however personal and private, appears permanently on one's digital record for all to see. When Facebook or other tech companies claim the right to use your personal information for business purposes, it is easy to see how distorted the issue of privacy has become.

Does our concern with protecting kids from normal child and adolescent errors in judgment have to fundamentally change because a twenty-something tech entrepreneur invents a technology platform with virtually no privacy standards? Are we that submissive and gullible as a society? Do we really have no ways to appropriately handle this technology development and allow kids to be kids? Does an overriding concern about a few people in Silicon Valley making billions on their IPOs prevent us from enacting clear, universally understood privacy standards and codes of conduct? Do we really believe that the brilliant technology gurus, who are coining money on these platforms, can't come up with an "eraser" button that would protect our kids' reputations over the long term? Why are we so passive about this topic when the implications of privacy are so meaningful for the social and emotional well-being of our kids and families?

The Lack of Privacy Standards and Leadership

The current state of privacy law and regulations in the United States is like the Wild West. Any rules and standards, if they exist, are made to be broken, and it's not even clear who the sheriff is. In this vacuum, tech companies have essentially defined most of the rules, whether we like it or not. People reveal personal data on the latest app or social network, and this data is essentially the oil that greases the Internet. Then companies aggregate the information and think up the most inventive ways to use it for potential profit. Users' behavior is tracked and analyzed from every conceivable angle, and companies like Facebook alter or modify their privacy policies frequently. Most consumers, especially young people, have no clue what privacy policies cover in the first place. In short, it's an industry-wide problem with enormous implications for all of us.

One glaring example of the lack of effective privacy oversight in the United States was Facebook's introduction of facial recognition technology. The software scans new photos that users upload, then compares the faces in the pictures with previously labeled photos to see if it can find a match. If there is a match, Facebook invites the person who uploaded the photos to tag the other people in the picture. Facebook's apparent rationale for this new product was that it could speed up the process of labeling and identifying people in photos, which is a central feature of their platform. This feature is automatically enabled. To disable it, users must navigate Facebook's byzantine privacy controls.

As has been its customary practice, Facebook gave its customers little meaningful notice of this privacy-invading product, and U.S. regulatory authorities were initially mute about it. Users, however, began to object to this feature when they realized that it was automatically enabled, and

European officials recently announced a formal investigation into the practice. Earlier, European regulators had also forced Facebook to change its "Friends Finder" application, which allows Facebook to copy a user's e-mail address book in order to identify "friends" who are on Facebook— with scant notice to the user whose e-mail data was being gathered and mined.

Sadly for those of us who live in the United States, European officials have been far more vigilant and aggressive than our own government in defending consumer privacy protections against these technologies. European regulators have also sought to protect consumer rights on such issues as online mapping, geolocation services linked to cell phone advertising, and other social network features. In addition, European privacy advocates have been far more effective in getting government to protect the consumers' interests. Where is the leadership from their U.S. counterparts?

In 2010, for example, Google was forced to apologize to privacy regulators around the globe and was sanctioned with fines after reports made it clear that its fleet of Street View mapping vehicles were also collecting reams of private data from unencrypted Wi-Fi systems. Google tried to explain this unauthorized accumulation of personal data as a "programmer's error."[12] But the lesson of this incident is clear. Giant tech companies are collecting and storing large amounts of very personal information about you and your family, often without your knowledge or permission. Who is to say what they will do with that private information? And don't you and your children have the right to know about these practices and prevent them?

Two incidents in 2011 further illustrate how large companies are violating consumers' basic privacy without their knowledge. In April, researchers showed that Apple's iPhones and iPads were storing lots of data about their users' locations and personal movements. The researchers also showed how this data could then be used to track users' recent travel and whereabouts and produce targeted, unsolicited ads. It was a total Big Brother scenario, and Apple quickly issued a statement acknowledging two "bugs" related to information storage and said it never plans to track users' "iDevices." Shortly afterward, Sony admitted that its massive Play-

Station network had been hacked, resulting in a very troubling breach of personal data.[13] The hackers accessed a Sony database that contained the names and addresses, credit card numbers, and computer passwords of more than 2 million Sony customers. The hackers were apparently interested in selling this personal information for profit, and this latest privacy transgression temporarily took Apple off the hot seat.

These examples underscore the fact that privacy issues are a huge, growing concern for all of us. Large corporations like Facebook, Google, Sony, and others feel empowered to collect and use your personal information as they see fit, from your location and shopping patterns to addresses, credit card data, and personal photos. When confronted, their response is "Trust us," or "This is for your benefit." They assert that this provides a better advertising experience. But consumers and government officials should not blindly accept that answer, especially when it comes to kids and teens. As I will discuss later in this book, it is time for all of us to stand up and demand that our privacy be respected.

When your average thirteen-year-old gets an iPhone today—and I am not recommending that!—here's what typically happens. He sets up accounts on, say, Facebook and the Pandora music service and downloads a few of his favorite game apps. Right then and there, he has already given up a lot of private information that you might not be happy about. The app games are likely tracking his personal location because he has probably enabled their GPS feature. He has also had to surrender his parents' credit card information in order to purchase the apps, and iTunes, of course, has his family's account information, including names and e-mail addresses. The apps also share personal information, such as your unique device ID, with advertisers. Facebook knows your kid's birth date, his school, and most likely a trove of other personal data and photos documenting his and his friends' lives.[14]

Your average thirteen-year-old probably never stops for a minute to think about what privacy means or how private information can be used to exploit him in various ways. There's little chance that he's actually read Facebook's latest privacy policies. And it's doubtful that his parents have set the complex controls on his phone before he began using it and surrendering his private information to large companies that want to make money off him. If he's your average seventh-grader, he's given up all that personal data without any meaningful understanding of his legal right to and need for personal privacy.

What makes this pattern worse is that the tracking and profiling of children has become a widespread, global practice. The *Wall Street Journal,* for instance, reported in the fall of 2010 that 4,123 "cookies" and other types of online tracking technology were installed on a test computer used specifically to visit the top fifty websites used by children and teens. This was 30 percent more "cookies" than those found in a similar *Wall Street Journal* test of the fifty top overall sites, which mainly targeted adults.[15]

In the face of this rampant tracking, kids have very few privacy protections, and the current law is hopelessly outdated. The existing kids' privacy law in the United States, the Children's Online Privacy Protection Act (COPPA), was passed in 1998, when Mark Zuckerberg was in grade school and Twitter, Zynga, and Google didn't exist. As I've explained, COPPA prohibits the collection of "personally identifiable" information—including name, phone number, e-mail or street address, and social security number—from children ages twelve and under without parental consent. COPPA is currently the only significant national law protecting children's online privacy, and there is zero privacy protection for kids thirteen and older. One recent survey of parents that was funded by Microsoft provided some interesting data about how COPPA rules relate to Facebook. A great majority of parents (89 percent) believe that there "should" be a minimum age to join the service, and the average age suggested by those parents was 14.9 years. Even larger numbers of parents (93 percent) said that they ought to have the "final say" about a child's ability to use an online service. The survey also showed, however, that approximately a third (36 percent) of the parents polled reported that their child joined Facebook before the age of thirteen, and two-thirds of those parents (68 percent) helped their child create the account to avoid the age limitations.[16] FTC commissioner Julie Brill commented on this aspect of the survey, noting that "the fact that they are involved in assisting their kids to set up Facebook accounts indicates they want what COPPA seeks to provide—the power to hold their children's hands as they learn to make choices about how to share data online."[17]

What seems clear to me overall is that parents still want to be involved with their kids' privacy and social network choices. However, the huge changes in digital technology and media since 1998 make COPPA woefully out of date. New legislation is needed. Indeed, the law has been criticized by everyone from kids advocacy organizations to academic experts to the tech industry itself. The Federal Trade Commission (FTC), under the leadership of its thoughtful chairman, Jon Leibowitz, is finally trying to update some of the law's provisions and has recently issued important new additions to the COPPA regulations, but in general, our national commitment to kids' privacy has been a bad joke.

In late November 2011, the FTC and Chairman Leibowitz took the first major step toward sanctioning Facebook for its repeated privacy violations. The widely publicized settlement stemmed from a series of changes that the company made to its privacy settings in December 2009. These changes, which Facebook sprang on its users with little warning, made various aspects of users' profiles—such as their name, photos, gender, and "friends" lists—public by default. In what the *Wall Street Journal* characterized as an "aggressive complaint," the FTC accused Facebook of threatening the "health and safety" of its users by exposing "potentially sensitive affiliations," such as users' sexual orientation, business dealings, and political views. The FTC charged that Facebook's actions amounted to "unfair and deceptive" behavior.

Under pressure from the FTC and a growing chorus of consumer advocates, Facebook agreed to a twenty-year privacy settlement that requires the company to ask its users for their permission before changing the way their personal information is released. As part of this landmark sanction by the FTC, Facebook also agreed to submit to independent audits of its privacy practices every two years. Moreover, if Facebook violates the settlement, the company can now be fined $16,000 per day per violation. In essence, this agreement forces Facebook to allow its users to "opt in" to any new privacy changes going forward, rather than forcing users to turn them "off" after the company has unilaterally changed its practices.[18]

This historic rebuke to Facebook hopefully marks a major turning point in the entire privacy debate and in Facebook's conduct in particular. While the settlement does not punish Facebook for its past violations and innumerable privacy changes, it establishes the opt-in standard and puts the company on notice that at least the Federal Trade Commission will begin to enforce common sense privacy standards. Mark Zuckerberg responded to the settlement in a blog post where he admitted "a small number of high-profile mistakes" and committed to giving users the tools they need to control how their information is released going forward. We shall see.

The FTC settlement marks a major milestone, but it remains to be seen whether Congress will finally pass much-needed new privacy laws, especially concerning kids and teens. For most of the past decade, lawmakers on both sides of the aisle have been MIA on the privacy issue unless it affects them personally. In this vacuum, companies like Facebook built new platforms, fundamentally changed their practices, and eviscerated long-held societal norms about privacy. No new laws or regulations were passed to protect children and families. Meanwhile, way too much regulatory and legislative attention was focused on the tiny number of online predator cases that dominated our initial response to the Internet. While our timid, often ill-informed leadership in Washington and the state capitals twiddled their thumbs, the news media was fawning over the tech giants. Mark Zuckerberg, Larry Page and Sergey Brin of Google, and the MySpace founders, for example, were lionized as heroes and put on the cover of magazines like *Time* and *Newsweek*.

In 2011, to counter this gaping policy vacuum, Common Sense Media helped introduce bipartisan legislation—a "Do Not Track Kids" bill—that would significantly bolster children's privacy protections and prevent online tracking of kids and teens. The proposed legislation would ban "behavioral marketing" and geolocation monitoring of youngsters without a formal and explicit opt-in by their parents, as well as a formal opt-in for older teens. Today, many companies freely troll the Internet and digital cell phone data to collect kids' detailed personal information, then target them with behavioral marketing that is specifically tailored to their age, gender, and interests. This proposed bipartisan legislation correctly views that practice as "deceptive and unfair" to kids and would eliminate its widespread use and abuse.

In addition, this proposed legislation would require technology giants to create and distribute an "eraser" button for kids, teens, and hopefully all consumers. Web companies should make it possible for young people to completely delete personal information that they regret having posted or shared publicly. No thirteen-year-old should have to live the rest of his or her life with the consequences of some poor, impulsive decision that was shared online. This is the very least society should ask from an industry that has repeatedly created ingenious ways to challenge norms of privacy and personal behavior. Alas, as I write this in early 2012, the "Do Not Track Kids" legislation remains stalled in the partisan politics of Washington, under intense lobbying pressure by industry representatives. Organized public pressure is clearly one of the next steps we need to move it forward.

Common Sense and many other leading organizations strongly assert that the universal industry standard for all privacy decisions by consumers should be "opt in"—as opposed to the confusing "opt out" standard that was contrived by the tech industry for commercial gain. We recognize, as the U.S. Supreme Court consistently has, that privacy is a fundamental right for American citizens and that consumers should have to formally give their explicit consent—officially "opt in"—before their private, personal information is used by others for commercial purposes. Industry privacy policies and requests for permission to use private information should be simple, understandable, and clear.

You might wonder why these common sense privacy laws aren't already on the books. The answer is depressingly simple: money and corporate power in our dysfunctional political system. While large tech companies were inventing products that reshaped our lives and the landscape of personal privacy, they were also hiring legions of lobbyists and lawyers to represent their interests in Washington, D.C. Tech leaders aren't dumb.

They know how our political system works, and they know that money and political favors talk.

Put simply, our government leaders need to do the jobs for which we elected them. They need to pass strong and enforceable privacy legislation and create a common sense regulatory framework that will balance the needs for technological innovation and entrepreneurship with critically important privacy protections for all consumers, but especially for young kids and teens. Our elected officials have been slow to enter the fray, but the time for a thoughtful, balanced privacy framework is now. From President Obama—who steers his own daughters away from having Facebook accounts[19]—to leaders on both sides of our dysfunctional political aisle, the need for strong, bipartisan leadership on this issue could not be clearer. Despite the millions spent by the tech industry on D.C. lobbyists and lawyers, who seek to block, or at the very least water down, reasonable privacy protections for kids and consumers, all of us will benefit from them in the long run—including, I believe, the tech industry itself. These companies will benefit from a strong privacy framework, because a safe, consistent digital environment will protect all of us. Moreover, it will ultimately encourage parents and young people, who feel comfortable with proper privacy protections, to make even wider use of appropriate online platforms.

The tech industry has to be held accountable and required to do its part to protect our privacy. To date, the industry titans and "weberati" have gone to great lengths to avoid a serious privacy debate and frame the issue in their own best interests—that is, profit maximization. This stonewalling needs to stop. We need enlightened industry leaders to step forward and behave as responsible parents and citizens. And we need the tech industry to use its extraordinary talents and brilliant creativity to create simple tools like an "eraser" button so that we can all live in this digital era without having to fear irreversible damage to our lives because of a silly mistake we made at age fourteen, forty, or sixty-five.

Parents need to be educated and involved, and we must stand up for our own and our children's basic privacy rights. Common Sense and other leading organizations need to conduct sustained public education campaigns to reach families across the country with important information about protecting personal privacy. We need to establish simple "rules of the road" to help guide everyone in the digital age, and our political leaders should require large media and tech companies to provide pro-bono airtime for these public awareness efforts. Finally, every school in the United States should adopt some form of a digital citizenship curriculum—like health ed and driver's ed—that teaches privacy protection and proper norms of ethical digital behavior from kindergarten on up.

All of us have a stake in creating a responsible, child-friendly privacy framework. Individually and collectively, we should make it happen as soon as possible and make sure that our voices are heard. Our kids deserve nothing less.

Chapter Four

The End of Innocence

Childhood is a sequence of revealed secrets.
—Neil Postman, media historian

Perhaps you've read or heard the haunting story of Kiki Kanni-bal, a fourteen-year-old Florida girl whose devastating rise and fall as an Internet "celebrity" was chronicled in *Rolling Stone* in April 2011. Before she began her notorious adventure on the Web, Kirsten "Kiki" Ostrenga was just another awkward, insecure teen living in suburban Miami. Then she got a MySpace account and started filling her page with pouty and sexually charged photos of herself. Kiki's images reflected her fascination with punky "scene kid" fashion. She named her new persona "Kiki Kannibal," and she quickly rose to Internet "stardom," with consequences that she and her parents could never have imagined.

Her dolled-up, provocative poses, in short skirts, underwear, and pink makeup, drew an assortment of bizarre, moblike responses in the online universe. Soon, her MySpace page was dominated by cruel, twisted, verbally abusive teens and stalkers. Kiki received death threats, saying, "I'll fucking murder you, little girl," and someone vandalized her home, painting the word "SLUT" on it in large letters. She also met her first boyfriend, "Mr. MySpace," through her Internet posing. This man later violated Kiki in her own bed before he was arrested on seven felony counts of statutory rape. It turned out that Kiki was not his only vulnerable, underage victim. "Mr. MySpace" subsequently died of injuries he suffered while trying to escape from police custody.

Kiki's nightmare went on for more than four years. During this time, her parents learned some hard truths about the seedy underbelly of the Web and for-profit teen exploitation sites like StickyDrama, which serve as go-to places for wannabe Internet celebrities. Her parents called in the police repeatedly and finally moved their family to escape the escalating dangers of online and offline harassment. They were also forced to confront their own parenting mistakes and naïve, permissive attitude about Kiki's "creative self-expression" on the Web.[1]

In a column about Kiki, *New York Times* columnist David Brooks wrote that online "eyeballs and page-views are king. Achievement is defined as the ability to attract attention. And, with today's technology, this sort of celebrity is not just a dream. Young people can create it for themselves."[2] But the consequences can be devastating and unexpected. Whether we want to admit it or not, in our media culture today, millions of people follow the sagas of attention-hoarding celebrities like the Kardashians, Lindsay Lohan, Paris Hilton, and the characters in Bravo TV's *Real Housewives* series. In a bizarre way, these media stars have become role models for our kids, who mimic their behavior as they search for their own identities on media platforms.

Kiki Kannibal's story is a particularly dark one, but at Common Sense Media, my colleagues and I often talk to parents and teachers who say they worry that kids are growing up too fast, too soon. Boy, can I relate to that. I remember thirteen years ago when our eldest daughter, Lily, was five and came back from a playdate where she had watched her first Spice Girls video. Lily came into the family room, shaking her little booty and lip-synching her favorite Spice Girls song, "If You Wanna Be My Lover." That marked the moment when I was first exposed as a parent to the incredible powers of media role models.

Young girls today might consider the Spice Girls to be pretty tame in comparison to groups like the Pussycat Dolls ("Loosen up my buttons, baby . . .") or "role model" actresses like Miley Cyrus, who was seen pole dancing on stage at the 2009 Teen Choice Awards. The media industry actually has a phrase for this phenomenon. It's called "age compression." Marketers use this term to describe how kids at increasingly younger ages are modeling behavior that older children once did. Indeed, some of the fashion items and toys that were once deemed to be appropriate for teens are increasingly evident in the lives of preteens and occasionally even preschoolers. Lately we've seen some outrageous examples where the fashion industry is encouraging little girls to dress up as sexy adults. This form of "age compression" is particularly disturbing to child development experts when it takes on sexual connotations. Increasingly, younger children are modeling adultlike sexual behavior without having anywhere near the intellectual or emotional capacity to understand what they are actually saying or doing. Needless to say, psychologists and many parents worry about the impact in both the short and long term.[3]

Sex Still Sells

The noted American media historian and NYU professor Neil Postman famously explained that childhood was a "sequence of revealed secrets." With the development of TV in the 1950s, he concluded, many of these adult "secrets" were revealed. As television became the dominant source of information and entertainment, childhood innocence diminished, and kids' sexual activity, exposure to violence, and drug and alcohol abuse began to rise. On TV today, we now find pathetic reality shows like *Jersey Shore,* where Snooki and other "stars" compete to embarrass themselves. Snooki even got her own spinoff show on MTV. Series like *Gossip Girl* introduce ten- and eleven-year-olds to sex, drugs, and tons of antisocial behavior, and too many parents just yawn because they're so used to seeing it. These efforts to push the envelope have occurred as producers and networks try to break through the clutter of the five-hundred-channel universe and compete with the Internet, Facebook, and cell phones for young people's attention and the billions in advertising revenues that go with it. The truth is, many parents are more worried about Facebook and user-generated videos on YouTube than the content of TV shows. But for kids up to the age of eight, television is still by far the single biggest form of media that they consume. As a result, the messages and images they see on TV still matter profoundly to their social and emotional development, even if they're watching TV on a computer or cell phone screen.

We all know that kids today are growing up surrounded by sexual images and messages and that there's no way to completely shield them in our 24/7 media environment. Many of these images are played for shock value, some contain graphic sex, and sexual humor is a mainstay of adolescent entertainment. But in this digital age, anyone can be a creator of media content, and Internet porn is almost impossible to avoid. Kids are curious, and "porn" is now the fifth most popular Internet search term for kids age six and up.[4] My own kids have been spammed by porn and pop-up ads for porn sites without looking for this stuff. Needless to say, that's a totally unwanted and unfair intrusion on their childhood. My colleagues at Common Sense Media report that some kids develop a prurient interest in the sideshow and bizarre stuff, like midget porn or sex with animals. We also know that porn can influence teens' sexual activity. For example, a 2009 study found that young teens who are exposed to sexual media content (for example, Internet porn) are more likely to have sex or oral sex by mid-adolescence. The study also found a positive relationship between young teenage boys' exposure to sexual media and their likelihood of perpetrating sexual harassment.[5]

The uncomfortable truth is that most parents have to assume that their kids will at some point be exposed to pornographic images online. Sure, you can use various filters and blocking mechanisms, but even the best filters aren't foolproof, and your kids can go online using so many different platforms. The only solution is to equip them with tools and critical-thinking skills to deal with this exposure. It can be pretty tough to have a conversation about sexual issues with a six-year-old who's still in love with Mary Poppins, long before you expected to address them. Still, it's important for us parents, whether we like it or not, to talk with our kids about these images and issues so that they can develop healthy perspectives. If we don't educate our children about values, the media certainly will. Studies by the Kaiser Family Foundation and others have made it clear that kids learn a lot about sexual standards and behavior from the media.[6] Research also reveals that listening to music with degrading sexual lyrics speeds sexual activity,[7] and that boys and girls who are exposed to a lot of sexual media content engage in sexual activity at younger ages.[8] The media is like a "superpeer"; the more prevalent sexual situations are in popular media, the more normal they seem to young people.

The Impact of Digital Violence

Media violence, too, often shapes kids' behavior. According to the American Academy of Pediatrics, exposure to media violence through television, movies, music, and video games can contribute to aggressive behavior, nightmares, desensitization to violence, fear, and depression. Studies have also shown, for more than three decades, that media violence can help create an almost paralyzing sense of fear in some youngsters by depicting a violent world where aggression is normal. This effect is particularly strong in younger children, who cannot distinguish between fantasy and reality.

When I wrote my first book, *The Other Parent*, the nation was still recovering from the violent rampage at Columbine High School in Littleton, Colorado. The teenage killers had massacred classmates and teachers alike and left a videotape talking about their love of the violent video game Doom. They had even discussed which movie director, Steven Spielberg or Quentin Tarantino, would immortalize their bloody exploits on film.

There is no question that a steady diet of first-person video game violence is introducing millions of kids and teens to images and sensations that affect their reality. Whether it is RockStar Games' notorious Grand Theft Auto series or disgusting video games like Manhunt or Postal, a relatively small but extremely profitable segment of the video game industry has fed millions of kids and teens a steady diet of increasingly graphic and often repulsive violence. Women are portrayed as hookers who give blow jobs and get sliced up, and characters are shot, maimed, and decapitated in ever more graphic, lifelike depictions. When my colleagues at Common Sense create video montages of some of the more graphic violent video games for public hearings or legal and legislative efforts, I literally cannot watch some of the stuff. It's simply too gruesome. Moreover, because it is interactive, gamers personally and repeatedly engage in these repulsive actions on their gaming devices, but that's simply the norm for video games with ultra-violent and sexually violent content. Sadly, much of this content ends up on the Xboxes, PlayStations, and computer screens of young boys and teens who play these bloody games for hours on end.

For the past eight years, Common Sense Media has helped to focus major public attention and supported legislative action to curb the violent excesses of this extremely lucrative sector of the gaming industry. I first became interested in the subject when I was teaching a group of eleven-year-olds as a volunteer at a middle school in the Bayview–Hunter's Point section of San Francisco. Many of the boys were regularly playing the video game Grand Theft Auto, and several told me that they had purchased their copies at a local store. I was shocked. The game clearly included adult content, gruesome violence, drug dealing, blow jobs from prostitutes, and other X-rated material. How could these young boys get their hands on such offensive games?

At the time, the video game industry had already launched its own "self-regulatory" rating system, and Grand Theft Auto was rated an "M" for mature audiences. But clearly, this industry-controlled system failed to prevent those eleven-year-old students in a low-income neighborhood from purchasing it. In fact, there were no actual laws regulating the sales of games like Grand Theft Auto to kids. To protect them, we had to rely solely on the promises of the industry and the vigilance of parents, many of whom were uninformed. A bit of research revealed that this problem was hardly confined to San Francisco, so Common Sense Media began working with leaders around the country to try to prevent the sale of ultra-violent and sexually violent video games to youngsters. At every step, we were opposed by the very well organized and highly profitable video game industry.

It was never the intent to limit the creative expression rights of the game developers. No matter how inappropriate or disgusting some of the images may have been, developers and producers have the right to create whatever messages and video games they want. I teach constitutional law to students at Stanford, and I've long been a staunch defender of the First Amendment and its protection of creative freedoms. The only matter that we cared about was the *sale* of these ultra-violent and sexually violent games to children and younger teens.

In California and states like Illinois and Michigan, legislation was drafted and passed that sought to regulate the sale of these violent video games to minors. Eventually, the California law was signed by Governor Schwarzenegger and was immediately challenged in court by the video game industry and its legion of lawyers. As the litigation made its way through various federal courts, however, a funny thing happened. Suddenly the video game industry got much more serious about the accuracy and enforcement of its self-regulated rating system, and so did retailers. The public, and parents in particular, were becoming much more aware of the extremely violent content in some of these video games, and as a result of growing pressure, the industry began to clean up its act. Ultimately, the California law was struck down by a majority of the U.S. Supreme Court in the summer of 2011 on what I consider to be dubious First Amendment grounds. A majority of the Justices chose to view the law as a "speech" rather than a "sale" issue. I strongly disagree with that reasoning as well as with the current Court's other consistently pro-corporation rulings.

That setback aside, enormous progress for kids and families has already occurred. The industry has been forced to improve its rating system and dramatically crack down on the sale of ultra-violent and sexually violent games to kids. Moreover, parents and the broader public have become far more aware of the inappropriate content of certain games, and more parents now understand why so much violent content in video games and other interactive media platforms can have such a powerful and negative impact on children and teens.

The traditional media industry itself has also long come under attack for violent content from parent and consumer groups. Public concerns about media violence were a critical factor in the Motion Picture Association of America's (MPAA's) decision to create the first-ever self-rating system in 1968, as well as the federal government's adoption of the ineffectual V-chip technology in TV sets in the late 1990s. Leaders in the traditional entertainment industry have long acknowledged that movies like *Natural Born Killers* and *The Saw* can negatively impact young people and that violence is a public health issue for kids. Indeed, most top entertainment executives I know agree that violence is a real concern for families. A number of leaders openly acknowledge now that media and entertainment companies have a basic responsibility to address it. That said, violence, like sex, is clearly profitable, and media is a bottom-line focused business. As Leslie Moonves, the longtime CEO of CBS, acknowledged, "Network presidents don't keep their jobs based on the number of Emmy Awards. Let's face it; there is more sensation and violence because it works."[9]

The Myth About Sexual Predators

There are many ways in which digital media can steal childhood innocence, but the classic fear that many parents have about sexual predators— posing as kids in Internet chat rooms and luring their unsuspecting prey to meetings at malls—turns out to be overblown. An important national task force on Internet safety issues that was formed by state attorneys general across the United States released a report in 2009 debunking the myth of widespread predator problems. After extensive research by experts from Harvard University and elsewhere, the task force concluded that kids and teens were far less threatened by sexual predators than many Americans believed. "The image presented by the media of an older male deceiving and preying on a young child does not paint an accurate picture of the nature of the majority of sexual situations and Internet-initiated offline encounters," the report noted.[9]

The data show that concerns about online deception by predators—a horrific but rare occurrence—tend to overshadow more pervasive and important concerns like privacy and cyberbullying. In fact, one of the central elements of Common Sense Media's outreach to millions of parents and tens of thousands of educators has been to tone down the fear-based hype and emphasize education in digital citizenship and digital literacy. Although the Internet safety task force found that predators are a concern, the overwhelming majority of young people are not in danger of being harmed by an adult predator they meet online.[10] What this national safety task force did stress, however, was that "bullying and harassment, most often by peers, are the most salient threats that minors face both online and offline." Partly because researchers can't agree on the exact definition of these behaviors, the extent of this far more widespread problem is more difficult to quantify, but some recent studies suggest that as many as 49 percent of all young people have experienced some type of online bullying or harassment.

The Rise of Sexting

When my colleagues at Common Sense look at the data and hear daily feedback from parents, teachers, and young people around the country, one particularly common concern involves damaging self-revelation behaviors like sexting. People "sext" when they electronically send sexually explicit photos or messages. It's a practice that strikes me as the epitome of impulsive risk-taking in a world where childhood innocence has been compromised by all forms of media. The foolishness of thirteen-year-olds transmitting nude pictures of themselves over cell phones or the Internet never ceases to amaze me. Yet when you stop and consider that our kids are constantly bombarded by highly sexualized messages and images at younger and younger ages, perhaps it's not really that surprising. Think about the cumulative effect of sexual images that even young children see in advertisements, TV shows, movies, and music videos, as well as the random online pornography they may be exposed to, unwittingly or wittingly, on the Internet. Then add the provocative YouTube videos of young kids in highly sexualized poses, mimicking their favorite music video stars, and it starts to make sense that certain youngsters might believe that sending explicit images of themselves could make them cool or popular.

Our kids are exposed to so much sexual imagery at younger and younger ages that sexting is just a logical extension. We hear reports of this behavior as early as fifth and sixth grade now. When you consider that YouTube is the most popular video site for kids ages two to eleven and that many third-graders now have cell phones equipped with video cameras, the increase in sexting seems like a very risky but fairly logical outgrowth of trends in the broader culture.

What's a Parent to Do?

To me, sexting is just one more glaring example of how recent trends in digital media and technology have justified Neil Postman's comments about the disappearance of childhood. Sexting is contrary to the very core of the concept of childhood normalcy, and as a parent and teacher, I feel a palpable sense of mourning for kids' loss of innocence. Sexting also reminds me how incredibly important it is for parents and teachers to talk with kids, share their parental values, and help them make good decisions.

Before he died in 2003, Neil Postman said he hoped society would educate young people about the history, social effects, and psychological biases of technology, so that they could "use technology, rather than being used by it."[11] Our kids may indeed be living in a world of revealed secrets, but we can counteract this loss of innocence by teaching them good judgment and values. The good news is that we are actually beginning to have this discussion and open dialogue in homes, schools, and communities across the nation. Some of the issues related to media sex and violence have been around for decades, but we have done too little to curb them, and childhood norms have eroded as a result. Other concerns, like sexting, are very recent phenomena that have been greatly facilitated by the impersonal, impulsive nature of digital platforms. As parents and educators, we must highlight the excesses and inappropriate nature of some traditional media content as well as the forms they can take in this digital age of cell phones, Facebook, and Twitter. In general, we clearly must also hold the media and technology companies accountable for their contributions to the problems and insist that they be part of the solution. By doing so, we can give our kids the safer, healthier childhood and adolescence they deserve.

Chapter Five

Embracing the Positives of Digital Media

Technology is neither good nor bad; nor is it neutral.
—Kranzberg's First Law of Technology

When I decided to write this book, I hoped it would serve as a powerful wake-up call about the extraordinary changes in our kids' lives created by the new digital reality. I felt strongly that I needed to highlight a variety of concerns about how digital media and technology were shaping, and in some cases reshaping, the worlds in which kids are growing up. But from the outset, I wanted to emphasize a balanced approach—to make it clear that this new digital landscape presents both perils and possibilities. Moreover, I believe that it's up to each of us to use digital media thoughtfully and as a positive, productive motivator for kids.

In my view, the digital media revolution that we are experiencing has exceptional potential in three areas. The first involves improving educational opportunities and what leading educators call twenty-first-century learning—harnessing the extraordinary power of technology to fundamentally overhaul America's education system, especially our woefully outdated and underperforming K–12 public schools. Strategic use of technology and media can spur bold improvements in teaching and learning methods.

It boggles my mind to see how deeply and seriously this nation has underinvested in our children and schools during the past thirty years. To me, it is profoundly shortsighted and a national tragedy. In an era of increasing global economic competitiveness, what rational person or society would consciously choose to underinvest in building the educational capacity of its human capital and future workforce? And what is the inevitable outcome for cultures that fail to invest in their future generations and continually shortchange their educational systems?

The misguided priorities that have allowed our nation's public education system to deteriorate, and in some cases crumble, are morally wrong and economically insane. Yet that is exactly the scenario that has transpired in America during the past three decades. And the chickens have come home to roost, whether we want to admit it or not. Our nation's education system is broken. Millions of our children have been left behind, some permanently. There is no more urgent investment for America to make than to reform and rebuild our public education system. We need new, improved school buildings and new systems of learning that will help our kids prosper and grow in the twenty-first century. The good news is that technology and new models of "blended learning," when used wisely, can play an enormously positive role.

I recently heard a story, for instance, about a high school junior at a large, stressed public school in New Orleans. The student, Joaquin, lived with his mom and two younger sisters in a damp two-bedroom apartment with a sagging roof. He worried a lot about how his mom would pay for food. He wasn't doing well in school and was at risk for dropping out until, in a special ninth-grade English class that gave each student a laptop, he discovered that he had a great talent for creating music and videos. Once Joaquin found that computer—and with it, his unique creative gifts—his academic interest and performance literally changed overnight. Two years later, Joaquin is near the top of his class and applying to a select group of colleges. And both his mother and teachers attribute this remarkable transformation to his newfound commitment to computer-based learning and creative expression.[1]

Everywhere in America today, technology and media are being

integrated into our kids' school experiences. Bold thinkers like former schools chancellor Joel Klein and Mayor Mike Bloomberg in New York helped create and fund technology-centric schools like New York's School of One, where kids benefit from individualized resources and assignments in a personalized learning environment. In Southern California, new schools are springing up, like San Diego's High Tech Charter School, to prepare kids for the future. On the East Coast, innovative new thinkers are leading the charge for game design in classrooms. A technology entrepreneur, John Danner, has launched a national network of charter schools called Rocket Ship Education that stresses high-quality, individualized learning. Bold new models for "blended learning" mix face-to-face instruction with computer-mediated activities. The entire state of Maine is now making a laptop available to every high school student. The MacArthur Foundation's digital media and learning initiative, led by Connie Yowell, has contributed greatly to the field and has funded groundbreaking research on learning and student engagement. And the creative team behind *Sesame Street,* our friends at Sesame Workshop, have now created the Joan Ganz Cooney Center to develop new models of digital learning for younger students.

At the national level, Secretary of Education Arne Duncan has ranked at the very top of President Obama's appointments. He clearly values technology innovation and has made it an important element of his new agenda for public education. His top technology adviser, Karen Cator, who spent years at Apple, is working with educators across the United States to promote innovative uses of technology in the classroom. The chairman of the FCC, Julius Genachowski—a great friend and founding board member at Common Sense Media—has made digital literacy and universal broadband adoption a centerpiece of his national agenda for progress in communications. Together, he and Secretary Duncan have launched an important new national commission focused on education and the digital future. And this national initiative comes none too soon. Countries from South Korea to India and Brazil recognize and are investing heavily in technology as a centerpiece of twenty-first-century learning and education.

Young people are growing up digital today, and how we use these extraordinary new tools for educational purposes will help define this nation's future growth or decline on the global stage. Technology will never replace teachers, but we also know that it appeals to kids, and the Internet and broadband connections can benefit teaching and learning in many ways. A recent report cited student gains of around 10 to 20 percent in math, science, reading, and writing in technology-enhanced learning environments. In more and more cutting-edge schools, students are using their laptops and phones for everything from video production to basic research. Teachers are also increasingly using technology in their classrooms as a core element of the curriculum and a way to connect with students on familiar territory.

High school principal David Reilly in Woodside, California, believes it's critical to reach kids in the digital arena, where they spend so much of their time. He worries that they can become lost in and addicted to virtual worlds, but he also sees the potential for great new learning when digital tools are properly used by educators.[2] At Common Sense Media, we're seeing that more and more educators as well as parents across the country are recognizing the digital immersion of their children and are trying to turn this trend into a positive aspect of education. Where teachers and principals see new possibilities for learning, entrepreneurs see a market opportunity that can create personalized educational devices to match kids' different learning styles and capabilities. Start-up companies are now creating a whole new wave of interactive consumer products to tap this market, ranging from iPhone apps to learning games. This is the wave of the future, and we need to embrace it.

Many electronic games can provide positive experiences for kids and families, and millions of users have used CommonSense.org to find "the good stuff" in this genre. Although we have been highly critical of the makers and distributors of ultra-violent and sexually violent games, we see electronic gaming as an important new frontier for kids' education and entertainment. Games can promote new forms of teamwork and collaboration, and they can help teach youngsters deductive reasoning skills.

To some, electronic gaming can be an important entry point for technical expertise and media literacy.[3] Indeed, Common Sense Media has developed interactive gaming products, like our new Digital Passport, to teach millions of young people the basic "rules of the road" of digital citizenship. Colleagues like Michael Levine of Sesame Workshop and Katie Salem of Quest to Learn are also heavily involved in promoting games as an essential element of twenty-first-century learning.

At Common Sense, we have also responded to this growing intersection of technology and education by developing the first-ever educational ratings system, with the pioneering support of Susan Crown and the SCE Foundation. Our goal is simple: as companies and entrepreneurs increasingly create and market digital products that claim to be "educational," parents and teachers need a simple, trusted way to evaluate their educational validity. Since Common Sense has already established itself as the "Consumer Reports Guide" for kids and family media, providing consumers and users with similar ratings for educational technology products is a natural extension of our work. The growth of these platforms will undoubtedly be central to America's educational and economic competitiveness in the years ahead.

For more than a decade, I've argued that technology and media have an important role to play in kids' education. What's unique today, however, is that the boundaries between schools and home are starting to blur because of new technology. Teachers routinely ask students to do research assignments on the Web. They have students create mock social network profiles for historical figures or Wikipedia pages about the scientific concepts they're studying. Many educators now use "smart boards" and laptops in classrooms and design software for particular courses. Some even ask students to "follow" homework assignments on Twitter or to join invitation-only Facebook groups and pages to share presentations and information.

As Joaquin's story makes clear, many young people who are otherwise disengaged from school or traditional educational success can find their voice and passions in digital media. That's no small deal in a society where academic apathy can run deep among many teens. Kids often learn technical complexity through collaboration with online friends, and their personal media creation can mark a jumping-off point for the exploration of serious talents. The validation they get from online colleagues can be an important confidence booster for many kids. And for the truly talented, this skill building and creative expression can sometimes serve as the forerunner to future career opportunities and much larger audiences.

New digital tools and landscapes also offer young people a huge new palette for creativity and self-expression. Today, many kids find important new outlets for their creativity on the Internet and public platforms like YouTube. This has contributed to the new trend of learning anywhere, anytime. We are also seeing informal learning in after-school programs that use technology. When young people use the new widely available tools of video production and editing, their efforts can open up whole new worlds for storytelling, creativity, and imagination.[4]

Many parents view education as the primary way in which their children can prepare for the workforce, and increasingly, media and technology expertise and production skills are being translated into important career opportunities. As our society moves fully into the Information Age, growing numbers of young people believe that there's a potentially cool job awaiting them in the high-tech world, media, or marketing. While this often remains an upper-middle-class dream, the recognition of technology's central role in our economy and the job opportunities of the twenty-first century means virtually all kids now must learn the basics of digital competence and literacy. At the same time, this technical competence is increasingly relevant to their social life and cultural participation. Thus, two important digital trends are overlapping.

New research has identified three primary ways in which young people can be entrepreneurial in their media and technology pursuits. The first is by developing their creative talents, which can increasingly lead to artistic success and other career opportunities in publishing or media. The second is technology freelancing, where young people can obtain jobs and income through computer repair and IT consulting, for example. And third, increasing numbers of young people pursue online business opportunities or go to work for emerging Silicon Valley companies. I see this all the time among my students at Stanford. Online business is a nationwide trend that's likely to expand exponentially in the coming years.[5]

How our nation integrates technology into twenty-first-century classrooms will be absolutely critical to reforming and modernizing our antiquated public education system and giving our children the education and training they need to succeed in a global economy. There are few challenges more important for America at this critical juncture, and there's clearly no time to lose.

New Possibilities for Social Connectedness

A second benefit of the digital landscape is the potential for expanded social connectedness—the possibility of keeping in touch with other people in positive new ways. The recent book *Hanging Out, Messing Around, and Geeking Out: Kids Living and Learning with New Media*,[6] by the respected scholar Mizuko Ito and her fellow researchers, provides a helpful framework for exploring some of those positive social benefits. Many teens, they observe, basically "hang out" online, and their typically lightweight social contacts move fairly fluidly between online and offline activities. Teens also "mess around" online, randomly searching and navigating until something catches their interest. "Messing around" is different from the purposeful information research students often do when preparing a paper or homework assignment; it's more open-minded and allows for experimentation. By contrast, "geeking out" is a somewhat more expert and intense use of digital media, from gaming to the creative production of videos. To researchers in this field, all three types of behavior represent ways in which kids use new media platforms to relate to each other and build identities.[7] They can also enable young people to trade information and ideas in real time. Social networks like Facebook have become a common place to hang out for many millions of kids, and there can be lots of advantages to this. As the great Harvard educator Howard Gardner said to me, "If you're a kid who is a bit shy or different or has an interest in people who don't live in your neighborhood, then the potential for connection with kindred spirits in the world is geometrically greater with the Internet. . . . That's why some of the odd people in the tech world love it so much."[8] My own kids like to use Facebook and other Web platforms to keep in touch with young people they've met while traveling abroad. These tools let them share their lives and experiences more regularly (along with some cool photos) and are great examples of the positives of the new global connectedness.

Democracy and Civic Engagement

The third significant area of opportunity lies in the broadly defined area of global democracy—what academics refer to as "civic engagement and participation." As we've recently seen in places like Tunisia and Egypt, as well as with activist campaigns here in the United States, the Internet has remarkable potential for political and social change. Digital technology has the power to improve participation in the democratic process, especially among tech-savvy young people who use digital platforms like Facebook and Twitter to organize movements and spread concepts of free speech and democracy in repressive societies.

In 2009, my friend Alec Ross was appointed Secretary of State Hillary Clinton's senior adviser for innovation. His charge was to focus on digital media and global politics to define an agenda for twenty-first-century statecraft. In this role, Alec has worked with colleagues such as Jared Cohen, now a Google Fellow, to use the tools of social media and digital technology to promote democracy and other foreign policy goals. In one example, Cohen and Ross leaned upon the founders of Twitter to keep their service up and running when protestors in Iran were using it to help coordinate protest efforts against the repressive regime there.

As popular revolutions spread in the Middle East in early 2011, young people spearheaded their movements using Twitter and Facebook. Whether to the secret police or the local political machine, social media presented a huge threat to established powers. In Egypt, for example, one of the most important leaders of the movement that overthrew President Hosni Mubarak after nearly three decades of dictatorial rule was a Google executive who posted key messages on the Internet that helped coalesce the protests. Other effective uses of social media have fueled major pro-democracy efforts in Tunisia and other countries across the globe, devolving power from governments and large institutions to individuals.

Here in the United States, social media platforms like Facebook and Twitter have also become central media players in all sorts of political campaigns. This was famously borne out during the 2008 presidential campaign, when Barack Obama used a sophisticated online organizing effort that was spearheaded by Chris Hughes, a key founding member of the original Facebook team. Millions of voters, young and old, were reached via the Internet, and this effort became the standard across the country. Today, virtually all serious political campaigns have an online component, and President Obama held a much-publicized "Town Hall" on Facebook in April 2011. From the presidential elections of 2008 and 2012 to the slew of new nonprofit entrepreneurs using digital technology to tackle domestic and global concerns, civic engagement by young people is increasingly facilitated by digital platforms. Students have used them to participate in disaster relief efforts from Haiti to Japan and elsewhere, and young people in the United States have long recognized the value of new media to increase their participation in social change and community-building.

Many young people also get much of their news and information from Twitter, Facebook, and other social media platforms. In fact, both of these companies now proudly proclaim their central role as leading news sources. This trend, however, poses some serious concerns that have been articulated by Eli Pariser, board president and former executive director of 5-million-member MoveOn.org, which pioneered the use of the Web for progressive social activism. In his recent book, *The Filter Bubble*,[9] Pariser details his growing concern that the news personalization trends on Facebook, Google, and other social media sites can severely restrict how and what news is delivered to Internet users. As people become increasingly dependent on social media platforms for information, the streams of news and information they receive are becoming increasingly narrow and limited to their own preexisting worldview. It's sort of like the Fox News phenomenon on television. However, the "filter bubble" created by the personalization technologies of the Web is individualized, invisible, and not voluntarily chosen. Instead, it is driven by codes and algorithms developed by all the major Internet companies. The danger is that it skews the information you receive and eliminates diverse and opposing viewpoints. Pariser warns parents and teachers about letting kids get their news only from Google or Facebook, and he recommends media platforms that expose kids to multiple points of view, including those they don't naturally agree with.[10]

Pariser's analysis is invaluable for parents and teachers who care about civic participation and creating a new generation of well-informed young people. Yet there's also no question that the Web has opened up vast new possibilities for young people to become more socially conscious and engaged. As Alec Ross sees it:

> Young people with cell phones now have previously unimaginable publishing and distribution opportunities. This gives them powers they previously did not have and makes them more relevant and important civic and political actors . . . The twenty-first century is a lousy time to be a control freak.[11]

In the end, it is critical that we embrace the potential of the digital media revolution. The key challenge is to respect and encourage the innovation, creativity, and expertise of young people, while providing adult guidance and participation. If we succeed, the possibilities of digital technology will outweigh the perils, and, as my younger brother Tom always says when we take our children on new family adventures, "The kids are going to be all right. They can handle this."

Chapter Six

Kids Are More Than Data Points

For me, nobody explains the mind-set and perspectives of today's tech leaders and Silicon Valley "gurus" better than my longtime friend, the author and *New Yorker* magazine media and communications writer Ken Auletta. Ken has written about Google, Facebook, and media giants both old and new for many years. He has a remarkable ability to understand their psyches and to get them to speak on the record. A profile from Ken in *The New Yorker* is a mark that you've truly made it in the big time as a media or tech industry leader.

When I first talked with Ken about the key executives of the tech industry, the lightbulb finally went off for me. He had recently finished writing a bestselling book about the history of Google and was in the process of interviewing Mark Zuckerberg, Sheryl Sandberg, and others at Facebook for *The New Yorker*. To Ken, understanding their engineering culture was pretty simple: it's all about data. As Ken puts it, "To the guys who run Silicon Valley and the tech industry, data is virtuous. Data is golden. Data is King."[1]

I believe this analysis goes a very long way in explaining how the digital media explosion has occurred and why there's often such a gaping disconnect between the perspectives of tech leaders and the best interests of kids and families. For many of the engineers who lead Silicon Valley companies and the broader tech world, the bottom line is that the more data you collect, the more you know about people, and the more you can predict their behavior. Not coincidentally, the more data you collect about consumers, the more you can sell to advertisers. For engineers, just like mathematicians, data is the Holy Grail.

Theirs is an efficiency argument, pure and simple. Data is virtuous because data lets you analyze and predict human behavior more efficiently. This is the fundamental core belief that drives much of today's technological innovation, especially in the online world of digital media. But what are the implications of this data-driven world, and what are the consequences of this never-ending pursuit of data? How much do we actually want these engineers and their companies to know, and what are the ramifications of all this data collection and sharing, especially for our children?

In May 2011, when *Consumer Reports* released a study that revealed that 7.5 million kids twelve years old and younger were using Facebook, the widely respected consumer group called this "troubling news" and pointed out that this reality was contrary to the Children's Online Privacy Protection Act (COPPA), the current federal law regarding children's online safety, which prevents Facebook from legally signing up members under thirteen. Shortly after this report came out, Facebook's CEO and founder, Mark Zuckerberg, responded by saying that Facebook should challenge COPPA. He also made clear his overall belief that Facebook would be great for all kids no matter what their age or how young their developmental stage.

When I first saw the *Consumer Reports* study, I wasn't shocked. It's been obvious for several years that younger children, often as young as nine or ten, are signing up for this new platform and lying about their age, sometimes with their parents' knowledge. Since there are currently no enforced legal protections, and since Facebook's CEO apparently believes this to be a good thing, the massive numbers of children under the legal age on Facebook is a fairly predictable result, though a pretty scary one.

Of course, for Facebook, the earlier it gets access to a child's life and data, the greater the opportunity it has to start building "brand loyalty" and all the profits that come with that.

What the story really made me realize, however, is that we as a society are on a major collision course between the public interest and the self-interest of leading data-driven tech companies. Indeed, this is a clash between two fundamentally different worldviews, only one of which cares about the consequences for kids. Moreover, the outcome of this conflict will have enormous ramifications for society and our children in the years ahead.

Engineers solve math problems, yet they often don't recognize the human consequences of their work. Engineers and tech gurus today often ask the questions "Wouldn't it be *cool* if you could do this or that?" "Wouldn't it be *efficient* if we could just collect all that data and target you more specifically?" Well, perhaps it would be more "cool" and more "efficient," but whose data is it in the first place? And what are the implications of this mind-set, especially for a vulnerable ten-year-old who may share data and information about her personal life without being aware of the potential consequences?

Unfortunately, many tech industry leaders don't appear to consider the consequences of this fixation with data aggregation. For example, in 2004 Google announced it would digitize all the books in the world. That was a cool idea. But the company didn't bother to ask the permission of the authors who wrote those books. It saw books as merely data, not creative products authored by human beings. Google folks apparently failed to consider, or at least underestimated, the intellectual property and personal ownership issues involved—until they were sued by authors and publishers.

As Ken Auletta sees it, many Silicon Valley tech leaders and engineers "live in a very narrow tunnel." Tech companies, with their singular focus on efficiency, figure out brilliant new ways to collect data and anticipate a consumer's clicks. And, of course, their business models are based on this ability. The more a technology or social media company knows about you and the more data they have about your personal behavior and preferences, the more they can sell it to advertisers, who crave this kind of information. This business model, and their belief that more data will allow them to offer even *cooler* services and products, is the underlying rationale for the new "transparency" and "sharing" argument we hear from Facebook and others.

"What Won't You Do?"

Fifteen years ago, Ken Auletta wrote a fascinating book called *The Highwaymen,* which offered a remarkable insider's view of the various moguls who were competing for control of the global media and entertainment industries.[2] The book disclosed a great deal about their basic psyches and worldviews. It essentially revealed them as industry leaders who had split personalities, who bifurcated their personal and professional lives.

The book is a compilation of various pieces Auletta wrote for *The New Yorker.* One piece was built on a very simple but pointed question Auletta asked of these powerful media and entertainment industry leaders: "What won't you do?" What Auletta discovered about such media moguls of that era as Disney's Michael Eisner, News Corp's Rupert Murdoch, and GE/NBC's Jack Welch was that they somehow disassociated what they did at work from what they permitted in their own homes. They would not let their kids watch certain shows or movies at night. Yet by day, their networks and studios would go and make the very same shows and movies that they wouldn't let their own kids watch. These media executives simply didn't take responsibility for the effect that their programs and content might have on other people's children. Their focus on profit trumped all other concerns.

Fifteen years later, Auletta and I see a very similar split personality emerging among the engineers and tech industry pioneers who now dominate the online and social media worlds. Yes, they, too, like their enormous profits, rising stock prices, and record-setting IPOs, but they *truly* love their data. They justify their business actions and behaviors through the engineer's rationale that "data is virtue." In Mark Zuckerberg's case, they justify this massive fixation with personal information and data, not to mention its value to their corporate bottom line, by claiming that it's all about "transparency" and "sharing." Like the media moguls Auletta interviewed, too often they don't think about the consequences of their pursuits.

But what are the consequences of this unbridled pursuit of data and all the "transparency" and "frictionless sharing" that it supposedly engenders? What are the human implications of those nice-sounding words? Most important, what are the consequences of this for an immature ten-year-old or a vulnerable twelve-year-old or an emotionally troubled teen? The Mark Zuckerbergs of the world don't appear to have considered the consequences in any meaningful way. And perhaps this is predictable. They're barely beyond their teenage years themselves, and many of them are not parents yet. Many of them appear to believe in a largely libertarian approach to life. And virtually all of them are engineers who pray at the sacred altar of data.

Perhaps you think I'm overstating this point, but just consider some of the absurd statements that Zuckerberg and other tech industry gurus make on a regular basis about personal privacy. Eric Schmidt, the former Google CEO, said that in the future, young people could simply change their names to escape their online histories. Reid Hoffman, the founder of LinkedIn, asserted that today's concerns about privacy tend to be "old people issues."[3] Zuckerberg talks of "evolving social norms," and he claims that Facebook wants to increase the world's "transparency and sharing." He appears to genuinely believe this naïve mantra for everyone but himself. He's a very private person, and you cannot "friend" him on Facebook. The problem is that very few in the data- and profit-driven tech industry appear to be considering the consequences of all this "transparency and frictionless sharing," especially when it comes to children and teens who don't know any better. Their companies act like huge, unaccountable utilities, creating increasingly efficient platforms that seek more and more control of our personal information and data. But nobody seems to be asking how you can be a responsible tech CEO and a responsible parent raising healthy children at the same time. And nobody seems to be asking what many of the tech companies "won't do" in their constant pursuit of data and profit.

There is another striking parallel between tech leaders and the entertainment industry executives of the 1990s. Historically, leading executives and companies in the traditional broadcast and media industries had remarkable influence over politicians in Washington and elsewhere because media had such an incalculable impact on election campaigns. Similarly, today's tech leaders increasingly hold sway over the very politicians who are supposed to rein them in on behalf of the public interest. Not only is Silicon Valley a gold mine of campaign cash in 2012 and beyond, but candidates for public office, from president on down, now conduct social media campaigns on Facebook, Twitter, and other platforms. So their political fortunes are now increasingly intertwined with their relationships to many of the giant tech companies and their top executives, just as they have been with more traditional media companies.

Do you think it is an accident that no serious children's privacy legislation has been passed by Congress since 1998? Do you find it surprising that politicians on both sides of the political aisle repeatedly fawn over visits from leading tech and social media executives? Do you think it is merely by chance that Facebook, Google, and others have massively increased their use of Washington, D.C.–based lobbyists and lawyers at the very same time as they increasingly claim control over your and your children's personal data and private information? Just take a look at how Facebook has hugely expanded its D.C. presence and PR efforts in the last year or two. I would suggest that none of this is a coincidence. Indeed, it is very similar to the cozy relationships between leading politicians and the traditional media companies and their top executives that have existed in our nation's capital for years.

Taking Back Control of Digital Media

The reason it is so important to understand who the new tech industry moguls are and how they relate to our lives and national politics comes down to one simple word: accountability. The more that digital media shapes our lives and those of our children, the more we need accountability from the engineers and executives who dominate the tech industry. They must also be part of any solution. Digital media and the vast changes it brings, both pro and con, are here to stay. It is up to each of us as parents, educators, and citizens to insist that the tech industry play a central role in expanding their many positive and pro-social opportunities while limiting their negative consequences. Significant change will only come about when individual leaders in this industry recognize that shareholder value and the related pursuit of data and efficiency are not the only values that matter.

Our elected leaders, and each of us, should insist on a clear code of ethics and social responsibility for the technology companies that hold such sway over children's lives. In the broadcast era, for example, the public interest responsibilities of the media industry were clearly stated, and large media companies were both proactive in pursuing them and held accountable by government and citizens when they did not. That's what led to the Children's Television Act of 1990. This set of public interest responsibilities has diminished during the past three decades of massive deregulation, but many traditional media industry leaders still recognize their obligations to the public good.

But no such clear standards and accountability mechanisms exist in the digital technology space. That has to change. This is particularly important since so many of the pioneers and leaders of the field are so young and have not yet embraced any meaningful sense of public interest responsibilities. Giants of the field like Bill Gates, Brian Roberts of Comcast, John Chambers at Cisco, and Tim Cook of Apple should set an example for these young tech pioneers. At the same time, several of the new generation of leaders like Larry Page at Google, Mark Zuckerberg at Facebook, Mark Pincus at Zynga, and Jack Dorsey at Twitter need to step forward and assume the mantle of leadership on social responsibility. After all, many of them are parents, too, and their platforms are affecting the lives and healthy development of millions of children, including their own.

In a related vein, our political leaders need to get their heads out of the sand and establish an overall framework for social responsibility in the digital age, with major new laws and regulatory standards that safeguard the privacy of kids and consumers. The technology industry has shown little concern or responsiveness in this critical area except when pressured by government. Thus, the path forward seems clear. Federal and state government leaders need to pass new privacy statutes and consumer protection regulations—now. And key agencies like the FCC and the FTC need to enforce them consistently, especially where the well-being of children and teens is involved. At the state level, attorneys general need to use their enforcement powers to hold the tech industry to account for the protection of young people and other consumers. With the current dysfunctional partisanship that dominates Washington, D.C., some of the most important government leadership in this area is likely to come at the state and local level.

There are some enormous legislative battles yet to come on the privacy front, especially where kids and teens are involved. It is the responsibility of our government officials to protect the interests of the most vulnerable in our society on many levels. In that regard, one area that will clearly need attention in the years ahead is the potential reemergence of the "digital divide." For example, a major Common Sense research study in late 2011 revealed a growing "App Gap" between upper-income families that downloaded educational apps onto devices like iPads and lower-income families that did not or could not do this for their children. This divide can potentially limit opportunities for full participation by low-income children and families in some of the most promising aspects of the digital age. Needless to say, government leaders have central responsibility for ensuring that this critical form of social inequality does not persist in years ahead, and industry has a huge part to play.

Ultimately, many of the most important challenges of this new digital era will only be met through sustained education efforts. Once again, both our government leaders and the tech industry must play crucial roles. First, digital literacy needs to be promoted in every home and school in the nation. This will necessarily involve both ongoing public dialogue as well as broad public awareness campaigns about responsible digital behavior and how to take advantage of important digital opportunities. These national education and public awareness campaigns must involve both public and private sector leadership. The White House, the Department of Education, and the FCC can set an overall framework for universal digital literacy, and the industry should be required to pay for and distribute key public education messages and campaigns. This is exactly the type of public–private partnership that benefits everyone, from our BlackBerry-using president on down. And the need for sustained public leadership as well as an ongoing national discussion of these issues couldn't be clearer.

Schools have an absolutely central role to play in transforming our system of public education and in teaching the basics of digital literacy and digital citizenship to every student in this country. But they can't do that alone. They will need far greater support from our government leaders and the technology and media industries, which will have much to gain in the long run. At the end of the day, however, parents are the first line of defense when it comes to their kids. Parents are both teachers and role models in our digital age. Those aren't always easy tasks, but they're essential. That's why the second part of this book is packed with practical parenting advice.

As the father of four kids, I frequently turn to my far wiser colleagues at Common Sense Media for basic advice and counsel about digital media. I'm fortunate to have their wisdom and expertise as a daily resource and guide, and I think my wife and kids have benefited greatly in the process, though our three teenagers might not always acknowledge it. Most of the challenges and opportunities vary greatly from babies to teens, however, so I've framed the advice and resources in the next part of this book by age and stage. Some tips, though—like limiting the amount of time your kid spends in front a screen—are just as essential for tots as they are for teens, and you'll see that I've reinforced and repeated them in several chapters. Whether you have a toddler, a first-grader, or a teenager in high school, the new digital landscape is a huge part of your child's reality. The next section will help you navigate this brave new world in ways that will hopefully benefit and inspire you as well as the kids you love.

Part II

Parenting 2.0:
Top Common Sense Tips

Birth to Age Two

The world is a digital stage when it comes to babies. Online audiences see their sonograms before they're born and their adorable first smiles and steps appear on the Web after they arrive. By the time many babies are just six months old, they already have "digital footprints"—indelible online histories that can stick to them like shadows as they grow up. As boundaries blur between public and private lives, it's up to parents, in a blizzard of technological change, to steer their children safely.

That's a challenging task. It's easy to be dazzled by new technology— iPhones and iPads and face-to-face Internet calls—that make it quick and irresistible to be in constant touch. A click of a mobile phone camera is all it takes to capture a moment in your baby's life, funny or wildly embarrassing, and share it with hundreds of friends and family members over social networks—it's so easy that a child can do it. Those photos are irresistibly cute, but they can also be part of your child's permanent, trackable, very public personal history. Will your baby be happy to discover them on the Internet when she's seventeen? It's something to think about.

It's also tempting for parents to believe that technology can make babies smarter and ahead of the curve. A big industry—what author Alissa Quart dubbed "the Baby Genius Edutainment Complex"—exists to make hefty profits off this idea. It spends millions of marketing dollars to convince parents that digital devices and programs can enhance baby brain development, giving them a technology-boosted head start in a competitive world.

But the reality, we've discovered, is just the opposite. When babies and tots spend time watching TV and other digital screens, learning actually slows. The truth, research shows, is that watching two-dimensional videos, programs, and DVDs distracts kids under two from the way their brains *really* learn—by physically interacting with you and other loving, three-dimensional human beings.

Babies and toddlers are naturally geniuses when it comes to learning. From birth to age two, their brains triple in size,[1] and they have an astounding ability to acquire language. When they're six months old, they can already recognize the sounds of languages they hear at home.[2] By the time they're a year, most kids have said their first words, and they're imitating and practicing new ones again and again, coached by the gazes, expressions, gestures, and exaggerated speech—called "parentese"—that grown-ups naturally use.

Baby video marketers say their products can speed up tots' ability to acquire language. But recent research starkly contradicts that claim. A 2007 study, codirected by Dr. Dimitri Christakis at the University of Washington, showed that, with every hour per day that infants spent watching baby videos and DVDs, they learned six to eight *fewer* new vocabulary words and scored 10 percent *lower* on language skills than babies who didn't watch.[3]

The reason babies don't absorb information from baby media, experts say, is that infant learning requires social interaction. Babies' brains are designed to learn from live, social human give-and-take, and they don't get that kind of sensitive interaction from digital screens. In fact, according to Dr. Vic Strasburger, pediatrics professor at the University of New Mexico's School of Medicine, watching screens likely interferes with crucial wiring that babies' brains are laying down in early childhood.[4]

So turn off the TV and computer screen and ignore all the marketing hype about baby media. The fact is, your baby's already a genius, and you're already the best-designed infant-teaching device ever invented. Still, since the world is filled with spellbinding digital products, here are answers and tips to help you make smart, common sense choices for your child under two.

What Parents Want to Know

1. How young can my baby be to start using electronic games, apps, and e-books?

These products may seem educational and fun, but they all have screens. So I would take the advice of the American Academy of Pediatrics and discourage TV and video watching for kids under two—and I'd also minimize all other forms of digital screen time.

Watching a TV, smartphone, video game, or computer screen has no benefits whatsoever for babies. Research shows that tots don't learn anything from screen media, and it may even slow their learning.[5] At the very least, it distracts them from the three-dimensional exploration, movement, play, and interactive activities that really build their brains.[6]

Still, I'm a realist, and I know that babies live in a digital world. They're surrounded by screens; 20 percent of infants already have TVs in their own bedrooms—something that I'd strongly advise against.[7] It's probably unrealistic to expect that babies will never spend any time watching a screen, but it's best to keep that screen time as short as possible. If you want to introduce your baby to an infant-oriented video game, app, or e-book, I'd look at it as another opportunity to interact. Cuddle up with your baby and read her an e-book or play with an infant app or electronic game together for a few minutes. In small doses, digital activities can be entertaining ways to help your baby learn new things—from *you*.

2. What specific types of programs are good for kids this age?

Reading to your child, in any format, is always great. A slow-paced e-book designed just for infants can be a good choice, especially if you turn off the narration and read it to your child in your own voice—pointing to pictures, repeating words, and asking your baby questions as you go along. Your infant can't see colors or follow a story line, but she loves the sound of your voice and the touch of your skin. The key is to pick an activity where you set the pace and engage with your child. Instead of focusing on a screen or machine, your baby's focused on you.

In general, though, the best choices for kids this age don't involve batteries or screens. Babies and toddlers learn by interacting with real people and by moving, manipulating objects, exploring, and doing.[8] They're the original mobile devices, and reaching, grasping, playing, and mimicking you is the best program for learning and growth—no batteries needed. In fact, if you want to boost your baby's brain power, the smartest approach is surprisingly old-school. Playing with blocks, it turns out, has been linked scientifically with high language scores. So turn off the gadgets and bring out a set of blocks to help your baby build the foundation for a strong head start.[9]

3. Is digital media helpful for a child this young?

Though marketers aggressively target parents who want to give their babies an edge, all the latest studies suggest that digital media is not helpful in any way for kids under two.

Watching TV, videos, or DVDs without parent interaction can slow babies' language learning, and studies have linked heavy TV watching before the age of three with sleep, attention, reading, and math problems.[10] The American Academy of Pediatrics recommends no screen time at all for kids under two. Even so, 90 percent of kids younger than two do watch their TV and videos, and only 35 percent of parents say they always watch with their child. For too many kids, the big-screen TV is a hypnotic babysitter that's isolating, unresponsive, and overstimulating their brains instead of helping them learn.

Parents, too, are often enraptured with digital devices and take it on faith that their babies and toddlers will benefit from using them. Scores of parents have posted videos on YouTube proudly showing their tots using iPads, computers, and smartphones. It's often fun to watch a kid acting like a grown-up, and in these videos, the parents seem to get a much bigger thrill out of the experience than the kids.

Too often, parents also *rely* on digital media to soothe squirmy babies and toddlers. Instead of picking up a fussy infant and comforting her with kisses and skin-to-skin touch, I've seen parents tuck an iPhone into the crib playing the downloaded recording of a human heartbeat. In a constantly connected world, they're missing out on a fundamental human connection with their own child.

Relying on digital media to calm and distract your kid—using TV or DVDs as a frequent babysitter or routinely handing your toddler your smartphone, loaded with It's a Lifeline! or BabySitter2Go apps, to quiet him down—can train your child to turn to digital screens, not human beings, when he needs comfort. That's the kind of emotional programming that, later in life, might be hard to change.

4. Should I worry about posting online photos and videos of my infant or toddler?

Social networks are a natural for sharing cute pictures of your little one with friends and family. If you've prudently restricted your privacy settings to the people you know and trust, there's little to be immediately concerned about when it comes to privacy.

But keep in mind that once a photo or a video is up on the Web, it stays up. Even if you delete it, someone else may have already downloaded and shared it online. It has a life of its own; it's out of your hands and part of your child's digital footprint—a record that's trackable, public, and permanent that your child will live with.

Another consideration is that digital photographs contain embedded information about when and where the shot was taken, data that can be extracted with computer software. As a result, more of your child's personal history is accessible than you might think. It's interesting to note that a number of leading tech executives don't post any photos of their own kids.

If you do opt to share baby pictures online, make sure that your privacy settings are carefully restricted and up-to-date. And think before you decide to post. That adorable picture might capture one embarrassing moment, but your child could be living with the uncomfortable exposure for a long time.

What Parents Need to Know

1. Limit screen time.

In your baby's first years, you're setting patterns and habits for the rest of childhood. And if there's one tip to remember when it comes to media of any kind, it's to limit screen time. That's important parenting advice at every age, whether your child is one, seven, or seventeen.

If your child doesn't grow up with the expectation that screen media is always available, on demand, he'll spend a healthier amount of time being physically active, exploring the real world, and interacting with people. And if you don't set a pattern of using screen media as a babysitter, you'll have a better chance of avoiding the habit altogether, to your child's great benefit.

2. Do your homework and choose age-appropriate material.

Before you turn your toddler loose with your smartphone, make sure you've test-driven the apps you've given her to play with. The same goes for any book, game, program, TV show, or DVD. Download it, read it, watch it, listen to it, play it, and gauge its appropriateness for your child, with these questions in mind:

- **Does it have educational value?** Screen media has no educational benefit for kids under two, but simple books and songs can help them learn vocabulary and numbers.
- **Does it have a positive message?** It's best to make media choices that impart positive values and expose your child to people from different backgrounds.
- **Is it sexy, violent, or emotionally intense?** If so, put it away or turn it off. The same goes for anything with profanity,

threatening speech, and scenes of drug dealing, drinking, or smoking. Your child is a sponge, and what he sees or hears he'll remember.

- **Is it a commercial tie-in?** You don't want your tot to get attached to cartoon characters whose real purpose is to sell a product.
- **Is the app a good match for your child's skills?** Little hands and fingers may not be ready for manipulating screen buttons or a mouse. Make sure the app you've downloaded is appropriate and accessible for your child so playtime doesn't end in tears.

3. Spend unplugged time with your child.

It's easy for our mobile, digital, constantly connected world to encroach on family time. We multitask all day, almost every day, and it seems efficient. Who has patience to do one thing at a time?

But parenting a baby or toddler is all about monotasking. You simply have to be patient, present, and undistracted to forge strong bonds of love and trust between you and your child. It's a slow process, and you can't do it while keeping one eye on your BlackBerry or the TV.

4. Technology is a tool, not a toy.

Digital gadgets are cool, and they're often expensive. That's something to think about before you download a lot of baby apps. Tots play with their toys by chewing and sucking on them, throwing them, and banging them against the table. That's a lot of abuse for a sensitive electronic device.

To protect your technology investment, one toy maker is marketing a smartphone case that surrounds the instrument with colorful handles, protects the screen against sticky fingers and drool, and features rattles and a mirror on the back side.[11] The truth is, most tots probably find the case more fun and fascinating than the phone.

But for parents of toddlers who are truly digital prodigies, there are other worries. If your child thinks your smartphone is her toy, she may demand it, yelling "Mine!" and have meltdowns when you tell her "no" because you need to use it. Precociousness is cute, and it's tempting for proud parents to encourage digital mastery, but addictive behaviors can start at a young age.

5. Make an agreement with your spouse and other caregivers about what's okay for your kid.

Once you've thought through these issues and determined what's best for your child, it's good to set some media rules. Then stick to them. It's a great habit for your family to get into and to start early. You'll get used to thinking seriously about media's effect on your child at every stage, and your kid will grow up knowing that there are limits to media consumption. A key step is to make sure that other caregivers understand your rules and respect them. Your baby will have the best start if all the adults in his life are on the same page.

Ages Three to Four

B y the time they're three and four, kids are curious, chatty, creative, and in constant motion. They love routines and repetition, and they're master mimics—watching and copying their siblings, friends, and parents as they learn and test behaviors, rules, and expectations.

Their motor skills are strong enough that they can use a fork, play with puzzles, and handle a remote control to turn on the TV or change the channels. They can also pop DVDs into video players and computers, take digital photos, open and play apps, and use a computer mouse. They learn from everything—active and imaginary play, music, stories, games, conversations, and digital media.

High-quality, age-appropriate DVDs, TV shows, and electronic games can be very educational for three- and four-year-olds . . . in minimal doses. The American Academy of Pediatrics suggests that kids this age spend no more than two hours a day, *total*, watching screens of all kinds, including televisions, computers, iPads, video players, and handheld devices. Small quantities of selective, high-quality screen time can help your preschooler learn shapes, letters and numbers, sharing, and cooperation. But the benefits depend on *what* and *when* he's watching and *how much* of it. Personally, I'd try to keep the total closer to an hour a day.

There's no shortage of great programming on PBS Kids, the Disney Channel, Nick Jr., and the Discovery Channel, and there are lots of non-commercial, educational video games for this age group on computers, Wii, and mobile devices. The right kinds of games and shows, in the right doses, can have positive effects. But the wrong kinds of media choices for kids this age, especially violent programming, can create problems. A landmark study by Dimitri Christakis and Frederick Zimmerman at the University of Washington showed that, for every hour per day preschool boys spent watching violent TV shows, they had three times the risk of developing behavioral problems at the age of seven.[1] This was true even if they were watching cartoons on commercial channels, which often have more violence than adult shows. Exposure to "cartoony" video game violence at this age can have the same impact.

So the first rule of thumb, when it comes to digital media, is to be very selective. Watch the shows, try out the games, and check out their ratings and age appropriateness at www.commonsense.org before you let your preschooler see or play them.

The second point to keep in mind is that timing matters. A 2005 study of kids age three to five found that evening media use of any kind led to lots more sleep problems. Bedtime media use, regardless of content, won't help your preschooler unwind; instead, it can lead to more nightmares and make it harder for your three- or four-year-old to fall and stay asleep. Preschoolers also have a lot more sleep problems if they're exposed to violent media during the day.

The third and most important point is to try to limit your child's total screen time to one-to-two hours a day. There are a number of very important reasons to do this. One is to reduce your child's risk of attention problems. A 2004 study of preschoolers showed that for each hour of television they watched a day, children had a 10 percent higher chance of developing attention problems at age seven, including restlessness, trouble concentrating, confusion, and impulsive behavior.[2] The cause, experts say, may be the fast-paced visual images in TV programming. Rapid-fire shifts in events and images may overstimulate and rewire preschoolers' developing brains and lead them to expect that real-life events unfold at the same speed. Tasks like learning to read and write, however, take time and patience, and children used to the instant gratification and fast-paced fantasies of screen media may get easily bored.

Your child's health is another huge reason to limit media. According to a 2006 study, preschoolers who are *exposed* to more than two hours of TV a day, even if they aren't actually *watching* it, are nearly three times more likely to be overweight. Being overweight makes kids vulnerable to a host of future health issues, including diabetes, high blood pressure, high cholesterol, heart trouble, depression, and low self-esteem. So limiting screen media, starting now, can be one of the best investments you can make in your child's health.

When the TV is on, kids are exposed to a barrage of eye-catching ads pushing high-fat, sugary foods, and the sheer volume of junk-food commercials can cause overeating. For example, a 2005 Harvard University study found that kids eat, on average, nearly two hundred more calories a day for each hour they spend watching TV.[3] And when children are sitting in front of a screen, they're not running, reaching, jumping, and moving around. It might be fun for a four-year-old to play with a soccer or basketball app or video game, but if he's doing that regularly instead of playing with a real ball, it could create an unhealthy pattern.

Many parents of preschoolers are well aware that too much screen time is a big problem, and they're careful to limit it to two hours a day at home. If their child is in day care, however, she could be spending much more time than that in front of a screen. A 2009 University of Washington study found that in 70 percent of home-based day-care settings, children under five watch 2.4 hours of TV a day. That means that for many preschoolers, the daily total can add up to five or more hours a day in front of a screen—more than one-third of the hours they spend awake. This kind of media creep crowds out real-life activities—reading, imaginary and physical play, and face-to-face interactions—that are crucial for your child's healthy development.

Media creep is often an issue with parents, too. It can be hard to unplug, turn off your phone or TV, and give your preschooler your full attention at the end of the day. You might be missing an important e-mail, the latest sports scores, texts from a friend, or your favorite reality show. But when you tune into digital media, use your Blackberry compulsively, and tune out your child, you're sending clear messages to your three- or four-year-old that you may not realize: that she needs to compete with digital devices for your attention and that being constantly connected, and often disconnected from the people you're physically with, is model behavior. Your preschooler is watching and learning from everything you do, even when you're not paying attention.

It's not easy to make the right media and technology decisions for your three- or four-year-old, and these answers and advice can help you make the best media moves.

What Parents Want to Know

1. Is it okay to let my three- to four-year-old play electronic games and apps?
Electronic games take players into alternate worlds that are colorful and compelling. Like TV, they have an addictive quality and compete with the real world for attention. For this reason, among others, I'd be very careful about getting your three- or four-year-old into the routine of playing electronic games and apps.

At this age, kids are laying the groundwork for a lifetime of choices and behaviors. If they're entranced by entertaining apps and video games now, they're likely to become avid gamers as they get older.

That being said, there are some great *educational* early childhood (EC) games and apps that can be fun ways for your preschooler to learn letters, numbers, and other school-readiness skills. If you play them with your child as part of her one-to-two hours a day of screen time, they can be good options.

The key is to be very selective. Choose educational instead of purely entertaining games and make sure they're high-quality and age appropriate. And keep all screen time, including use of apps and video games, to a minimum. Your three- or four-year-old may have the manual dexterity to swipe a touchscreen or wield a joystick, controller, or mouse, but he's much better off learning how to navigate real life than the two-dimensional reality, rules, and rewards of virtual worlds.

2. Can digital media help my three- to four-year-old learn?
The short answer is yes—if it's high-quality, age-appropriate, educational media in small doses.

There's a large body of evidence that educational TV shows like *Sesame Street, Blues Clues,* and *Dora the Explorer* can help preschoolers learn their ABCs, colors, shapes, numbers, vocabulary words, problem solving, and positive social skills *if children watch them in moderation.* Kids who watch them one to two hours a day can gain academic skills, but children who watch more than that may show declining achievement.

There hasn't been nearly as much research about interactive digital media, but the results seem similar. Electronic games and apps can help your preschooler learn if they're high-quality, educational, and age appropriate. Content and quantity are the key factors. Recreational games and apps—like Dress Up and Yummy Burger Mania—won't teach your three- or four-year-old any more than a cartoon episode of *Scooby Doo.* But there are hundreds of great educational choices for every platform—TV, DVDs, computers, and handheld devices—that can keep your preschooler learning and busy for short periods. You can find lots of recommendations at www.commonsense.org.

Remember, though, that digital media is no substitute for real-world, physical exploration and learning—from reading a book with you to fingerpainting, coloring, using plastic scissors, and playing with blocks, Play-Doh, and puzzles. Your three- or four-year-old may be a whiz at tracing letters and numbers on a touchscreen, but she also needs the manual dexterity to hold a pencil and trace letters by hand.

3. How do I know what kinds of digital media are right for this age?
The first thing to remember is that preschoolers should not be watching any adult programs or playing any adult-oriented apps and video games.

You may love playing World of Warcraft and DoodleBoy or watching *The Real Housewives of New Jersey,* but your three- or four-year-old should not be on your lap grabbing the joystick or playing in the room while your shows are on. Enjoy your adult media when your child isn't around, and limit his exposure to quality digital media made for preschoolers.

When considering electronic games, apps, DVDs, or TV shows for your child, keep these questions in mind:

- **Does it have educational value?** The best choices for three- and four-year-olds help them learn letters, numbers, basic vocabulary, simple science concepts like gravity, and basic social lessons, like how to share.
- **Does it have positive messages and role models?** Children this age soak up everything they see and hear, so positive messages are important. Adult characters should be dependable, and any bad behavior should have consequences.
- **Is it violent or scary?** Exposure to violence at this age can have negative effects on behavior and learning,[4] and kids' cartoons on commercial channels often have more violence than adult programming.[5] Avoid shows, movies, and games where characters use violence to resolve conflict. If your child sees that kind of situation, talk to him about other ways the characters could have solved their problems. And stay away from any content that could scare your child. It's not always easy to know what a preschooler might consider scary, but in general, avoid content that's emotionally intense, depicts parents and children in danger, and shows children being separated from their parents.
- **Is it sexy?** If so, turn it off.
- **Does it have profanity?** Bad language is a bad choice for preschoolers. They're sponges for new words, and they'll learn and repeat everything they hear.
- **Does it depict drinking, drugs, or smoking?** If so, it's not a good choice for your child.

- **Does it have ads or ties to a commercial product?** Three- and four-year-olds don't understand the difference between ads and other content,[6] and research shows that preschoolers are more easily influenced by advertising than older kids.[7] Free apps and electronic games are often loaded with commercial messages and product links, and lots of popular cartoon characters have profitable product tie-ins, like Spiderman and Dora the Explorer toys, that your child might beg for.

4. Is it better for my kid to spend time watching TV, playing video games, or reading e-books?

The top choice, in my view, would be to unplug and read a traditional, printed book with your child. The reason is that real books leave lots of room for your three- or four-year-old's imagination. They're also interactive—between you and your child, which is the best, most nourishing, educational kind of play.

That being said, there are moments—in the pediatrician's waiting room, at a restaurant, or when you're taking an important call—when it's great to have a digital option for your child. In those cases, e-books, in my view, are the best choices.

There are more and more high-quality e-books available, from digital versions of classics like *The Cat in the Hat* to new enhanced, animated, interactive stories like *How Rocket Learned to Read*. Three- and four-year-olds love poking characters on a screen and watching things happen or touching a word to make the narrator pronounce it. But all of the bells and whistles in some e-books can be distracting, and the experience can be a lot more like playing a game than reading a book. Still, as part of your child's one-to-two hours of screen time a day, high-quality e-books can be a fun way to get her to focus on language and play with stories and words for a little while.

5. How do I keep older siblings from exposing my three- to four-year-old to stuff that a preschooler's too young to see?

That's not easy. Older brothers and sisters often dictate media choices, unless you set firm rules that have consequences for breaking them.

So it's good to set media rules for your family and explain them to your kids, again and again. If your older son wants to watch a TV show that's inappropriate for your four-year-old daughter, ask him if *he* thinks the show is a good choice for his little sister. Have a conversation with him about it and help him understand that he has special privileges because he's older.

While you're at it, suggest some non-screen-oriented activities that they can do together, like playing outside. As a parent, you need to step in, lay down the rules, and actively manage your kids' media use, like other aspects of their lives.

What Parents Need to Know

1. Limit media.

This is the most important tip of all for kids at every stage, especially preschoolers. The earlier you set and enforce rules, the easier it will be to stick to them as your child gets older. It's good to teach her to ask permission before watching TV or a DVD or playing an app or electronic game; that way, she'll understand from the beginning that media use is a privilege. And make sure there are consequences if your preschooler breaks the rules—be firm and consistent—because there can be more serious consequences later in life when her media use becomes a habit that's hard to break. Too much TV, we know, leads to higher risk for obesity, diabetes, and heart problems. Too much time spent gaming and in virtual worlds can lead to attention, addiction, and relationship problems, depression, and a host of health issues.

So get your preschooler in the habit of spending very limited time in front of a screen, and make sure there is never a TV, DVD player, or digital device in your child's bedroom, since having one virtually guarantees that he'll be spending more time watching a screen. And make a real effort to limit your own media use when your child's around. Turn off the TV, since research shows that preschoolers who are in a room with background television use language less. Children also absorb TV's content and images, even if it seems that they're not paying attention.

So the best idea is to start limiting media use early. If you lay down the rules when your child is three, you'll probably have a lot more control and influence when he's thirteen.

2. Do your homework and choose age-appropriate media.

Before you let your preschooler watch a show or play an app or electronic game, check it out yourself and read its reviews and ratings. Don't fall for the marketing hype; decide for yourself if products and shows are really high-quality and appropriate for your child. Titles and manufacturers' age ratings can be very misleading. *Little Red Riding Hood StoryChimes*, for example, is a charming e book, but *iReading—Little Red Riding Hood* is a gruesome, cruel, and violent app that is totally inappropriate for little kids.

Watch out, as well, for hidden messages. Research shows that children's books are often heavily biased toward male characters[8] and that children as young as four associate thinness with beauty.[9] So look for media choices that encourage a healthy body image and avoid stereotypes. Three- and four-year-olds are already forming ideas about the world.

3. Be aware that marketers are aggressively targeting your child, even at this age.

On television, companies and brands bombard young children with advertising messages and branded cartoon characters linked to products and merchandise. Preschoolers are especially easy to influence, since they can't distinguish between commercials and TV shows.

Digital games and apps also give marketers exciting new access to "the preschool segment." Many "free" versions of apps and electronic games are loaded with ads, product placements, and sneaky marketing techniques, including in-game purchases. It's stunningly easy for your child to accidently charge hundreds of dollars to your credit card by poking at a few fun-looking screens. So make sure to set parental controls to prevent this. Unethical game makers are hoping to profit from the fact that young kids, and their parents and grandparents, aren't aware of these expensive traps.

4. Don't let your preschooler think that your smartphone or iPad is a toy.

It's irresistibly easy to hand your preschooler your pricey smartphone or iPad so she can entertain herself at a restaurant or in the backseat of the family car. But convenience can have a cost. Spills, drops, and sticky fingers can cause all kinds of problems with your expensive device. So can the expectation that your mobile technology is your child's toy, and that you have to share. Make sure your preschooler knows it's not a plaything, and that she can use it, with your permission, only as a special treat.

5. If you post photos and videos, don't share the names of your child or anyone else's, and check your privacy settings.

Your preschooler may already have a "digital footprint"—a permanent, trackable, online record—from the cute baby pictures you posted of him on your social network. If you haven't already changed your privacy settings so that only people you've designated can see your postings, it's really important to do so. Otherwise, anything you post, including pictures of your three- or four-year-old, can be seen by millions of strangers online all over the Web.

It's also vital, at this point, to be very careful about "tagging" photographs and sharing the names of your child and other kids. In fact, it's best never to do that for safety reasons.

Another tip to keep in mind is that search engines are becoming more and more powerful and that "facial recognition technology" exists that can instantly link photos of people with their personal information. The technology is not widely in use yet because of huge privacy concerns, but it might be introduced in the near future. It's another reason to be careful about posting photos and videos of your child and other kids. Many Internet company executives have a policy of never posting pictures of their own children. That may be the safe strategy for you as well.

Ages Five to Six

Five- and six-year-olds are exploring a bigger world. They're expanding their sphere from home to school, teachers, and friends, and they're making huge cognitive leaps, from reading to counting and adding numbers. They're also mastering physical skills like writing, swimming, jumping rope, and tying their shoes. Five- and six-year-olds know more, they can do more, and they're more independent. They're also immersed in a virtual universe of digital media.

By now, they can type their own Google search terms, ski on a Wii balance board, play Cut the Rope or Angry Birds on a parent's smartphone, and command the family's gaming system and remote control. They want to learn how to do what the older kids and grown-ups in their lives are doing, and they push the limits.

For parents, now is the time to get really serious about rules and boundaries. At this age, it's way too easy for kids to spend hours watching the tube on Saturday mornings or playing digital games on weekends or after school. The temptation is there—digital media's available, accessible, entertaining, and habit-forming. It's also an easy way for parents to keep their kids busy and out of their hair while they steal a little extra time to sleep or work.

But doing what's easy now, studies show, can lead to problems later.

Research suggests that when kids spend more than two hours a day in front of a screen—whether it's a TV, a smartphone, a PlayStation, or an iPad—they're at greater risk for attention, learning, and behavior problems.[1] When kids this age watch violent screen media, even cartoon violence, they're more likely to behave aggressively toward others. And when kids watch TV and play "free" digital games, they're often inundated with advertising for toys and junk food. Studies show that the more hours kids spend watching TV, the more likely they are to eat while they watch, eat what they see on the screen, and eat more,[2] giving them a higher risk for obesity and diabetes.[3] And if kids have frequent, easy access to digital media, from TV to handhelds and video games, they're more likely to become addicted to the fast-paced, impersonal, two-dimensional companionship of screen devices.

So it's crucial to set rules limiting the amount and kinds of media your child consumes. Keep in mind that a screen is not just a TV; it's also a computer and smartphone screen. I personally think that one hour a day of screen time is really enough. But it's important to decide, thoughtfully, what's right for your own five- or six-year-old, then set firm rules and stick to them. At this age, kids are learning to follow lots of rules—about manners, behavior, playing with others, sharing, and crossing the street. Rules about what, when, and how much media they consume are every bit as important to their physical, emotional, and psychological growth. Be aware that it gets much harder to set rules and limits as your child gets older.

As a parent, you wouldn't let your five- or six-year-old wander out the front door without your permission and without knowing exactly where she's going and for how long. That same kind of vigilance is what it takes to keep your child safe and healthy in the digital environment. The answers and advice below, and reviews and ratings from www.commonsense.org, can help you make the right decisions for your own family.

What Parents Want to Know

1. If my five- to six-year-old is allowed a half-hour of screen time, should he watch an educational TV show or play an educational electronic game?

Either type of screen media can have value, as long as it really is high-quality, educational, and age appropriate. By the time kids are ready for kindergarten, however, it's a little harder to find top-quality educational TV programs. Too many shows aimed at five- and six-year-olds are loaded with cartoon violence and commercials pushing sugary drinks, salty snacks, and other unhealthy foods. And studies have shown that when kids watch a lot of TV, they eat more, they eat while they watch, and they eat *what* they watch. So be very careful.

There are, however, some terrific educational shows on PBS Kids, including *The Electric Company, Design Squad Nation, Dragonfly TV*, and *Cyberchase*, that are commercial-free and great for kids this age. They're even more educational if you watch them with your child. Watching together is a great opportunity to guide, interact, explain, and encourage learning.[4]

Educational electronic games can also be a good choice, but again, you have to be selective. Well designed games can help five- and six-year-olds build cognitive skills, from reading to solving puzzles and math problems, but there are lots of games out there that are designed poorly or mainly for entertainment.[5] So do your homework. Watch the shows and play the games yourself to make sure they're right for your child and read ratings, reviews, and recommendations. And stick to your time limit, so your child has plenty of time to be active, to learn by doing, and to come up with his own creative, imaginative kinds of exploration and play. Consider setting a timer, or letting your kid know that he has "ten more minutes" to avoid struggles with turning off the game.

2. Are there educational media products that can really teach my kid at this age?

Studies indicate that high-quality educational media, in small amounts, can have a positive effect. Research has shown a link between watching educational TV programs at age five and higher high school grades in English, math, and science.[6] A study by PBS Kids found that three- to seven-year-olds who played the Martha Speaks game improved their vocabulary by more than 30 percent. Other research has shown that kids who used instructional software on a laptop, with teacher support, boosted their reading and math skills.[7]

So the answer is yes, with qualifications. The key factors are *content* and *quantity*. Studies suggest that purely entertaining media, violent content, and spending more than one or two hours a day watching a screen can have the opposite effect—*lowering* academic achievement and leading to attention, behavior, learning, and health problems.[8] So be very picky.

3. Is it better to build my child's reading skills using traditional books or e-books and digital games?
Encouraging your child to read is one of the most important things you can do as a parent. Reading boosts learning ability, vocabulary, and conceptual thinking and sparks your child's imagination. Reading with your child gives you both a chance to slow down, cuddle up, laugh, ask questions, and explore together. When you read to your five- or six-year-old, you're also teaching her important listening skills, and as she begins to be able to read on her own, she can read to you.

That's why, for me, nothing beats reading an old-fashioned, page-turning, printed book to your child. It's an interactive experience, between the two of you, that builds relationship, learning skills, patience, and imagination. You have to slow down and spend quiet time together to read a book in a world that's increasingly screen-focused, fast-paced, and fixated on immediate gratification.

That being said, there are some great e-books that can really engage five- and six-year-olds, help build their reading skills, and encourage their learning, curiosity, and exploration (see www.commonsense.org for recommendations). They're especially good if you turn off the computerized narration and read them to your child yourself. With all their animation and interactive features, however, some e-books are more like electronic games than books, and they can distract from the immersive reading experience. Still, from my point of view, they're a good second choice that can get kids excited about the fun of reading.

There are also a few well-designed digital reading games and apps that strengthen reading skills. But there's nothing like the quiet and closeness of reading a traditional book together.

4. Should my child use a special children's Web browser to go online?

Most five- to six-year-olds have already used a computer by themselves,[9] and some are interested in jumping on the Internet and exploring, like their older siblings and parents do. Obviously, though, the Internet is no place for a young child to explore alone and unsupervised.

Over the past few years, a number of developers have introduced children's Web browsers—protected, child-friendly Internet environments where kids as young as four, five, and six can click and explore safely, without parents having to worry about inappropriate content and contacts they may encounter. Some of these are better designed and more effective than others.

From my perspective, though, the best ways to protect your five- or six-year-old is to go on the Web *with* your child, for extremely limited amounts of time. Also, be sure to keep the family computer in a common area, where you can easily see what your child is doing; and make sure that you've set up age-appropriate filtering options on your Web browser. I personally wouldn't recommend encouraging a five- or six-year-old to spend much time at all on the Web when there's a real world out there to explore. And I worry that encouraging Internet use and independent browsing at this age could set the stage for digital addiction when your child gets older.

Still, for parents who want the added security of letting their child roam freely and safely in a kid-friendly Internet neighborhood, there are a number of good options that link only to safe, prescreened sites. Be aware, though, that some of them charge membership or subscription fees, and free browsers are often loaded with advertising banners and pop-ups that your child won't be able to distinguish from regular content.

If you're looking for a "Web-surfing with training wheels" experience, try out some of these browsers yourself to see if they're a good fit for your five- to six-year-old. Better yet, get out that bike with training wheels you have sitting in the garage and let her explore a bit of her own, real-world neighborhood, with your supervision.

5. How can I keep my kid from being exposed to age-inappropriate content?

Many parents have experienced the uncomfortable moment when they take their five- or six-year-old to a G-rated movie that has an unpredictably scary scene, or when they realize that he's playing a bloody iPad game with an older cousin. It may be impossible to keep your child from being exposed to *any* inappropriate content, but there are definitely things you can do to lower that risk and help your child deal with those encounters in a healthy way.

TV can be a big source of inappropriate exposure, especially if your child has an older sibling. Big brothers and sisters are rarely willing to watch a "baby" show geared to five- and six-year-olds just because their little brother or sister is in the room. This is where you need to step in, as a parent, and lay down family media rules for your older children. Let them know that there will be consequences if they watch an inappropriate show in front of your five- or six-year-old. Ask them if they think these shows are really okay for their little brother or sister, and remind them that they have different rules and privileges because they're older. Keep a library of recorded TV shows and movies that they can watch together, and if they can't agree on a show or DVD, suggest something else that they can do together—like play outside.

Movies can be tricky, too. Even G-rated films marketed for small children can have frightening scenes—especially these days, when producers often use violence as a way to add action or conflict to a movie. PG and PG-13 movies almost always have some violence, sexy scenes, profanity, or references to drinking and smoking that are inappropriate for kids this age. Your best bet is to read the movie ratings, reviews, and recommendations before you decide to buy tickets or rent the film.

The same goes for electronic games, apps, and websites. Read ratings and reviews and check the products and sites out yourself before you decide if they're age appropriate for your child. That's what www.commonsense.org is great for. And make sure you've got child-safe settings on your browser to keep your kid from wandering onto inappropriate Web content.

It's also important to speak up and be clear about what's okay or not okay for your child to watch or do when she's on a playdate or spending time with family or babysitters. And remember not to keep the TV on, tuned to adult programming or news, when your child's in the room. He might not look like he's paying attention, but he's really absorbing everything. If your child does see something that frightens him in a movie or show, give him lots of hugs and explain that it's make-believe. If he sees something that frightens him on the news, tell him that your family's there to protect him and make sure he's safe. And if your five- or six-year-old plays a violent video game, explain that violence is never an okay way for people to solve problems. You may not be able to protect your kid from all age-inappropriate material, but you can keep those moments to a minimum and use them as opportunities to comfort your child, reassure him, and teach your own values.

What Parents Need to Know

1. Be a role model. Set time limits for digital media use, for yourself as well as your child.

If there's only one tip you put into practice from this book, I hope it's this one. As a parent, one of the best things you can do for your child's physical and cognitive well-being is to limit her total screen time to one-to-two hours a day or less.

Let's start with the physical reasons. When kids spend more than two hours a day staring at or interacting with a stationary TV, handheld, gaming, or computer screen, they don't move enough, and they eat more. Those are two reasons why childhood obesity rates have skyrocketed in this country, tripling in the last three decades. A third of all American kids today are overweight, according to the Centers for Disease Control, and that increases their risk for serious health problems later in life, including heart disease and diabetes. So minimizing the amount of time your child spends watching a screen, and maximizing the time she spends playing, moving, and actively exploring, is one of the most important ways you can help make sure she has a healthy life.

Spending too much time with digital media can also lead to a host of other problems, including attention, learning, behavior, and sleep issues. In small amounts, with controlled content, screen time can be educational and entertaining, but too much of it can be as unhealthy as a diet of candy, sugary soft drinks, and french fries. Your child's media diet is as important as physical nutrition. Just like you control your five- or six-year-old's access to sweets and junk food, it's essential to control his access to screen media.

A crucial step is to make sure that your child doesn't have a TV, computer, gaming system, or handheld device in her own bedroom. Nearly half of all kids this age do. Parents may like having the ability to watch a different program at the same time or think that a device will help their kid fall asleep. The truth, however, is that kids who have TVs in their rooms have lower test scores at school, a greater risk of being overweight, and a higher risk of sleep problems, since TV watching stimulates alertness.[10] Remember the old real estate maxim: location, location, location. If your child already has a TV in his bedroom, it's a wise idea to take it out—the sooner the better, since it will get more difficult to do that as he gets older. And if you're thinking of getting a new flat-screen and putting your old TV in your child's bedroom, it's a better idea to put it in the basement or give it away. Studies show that older kids who have TVs in their own rooms are more likely to watch a lot more TV without their parents' knowledge, eat more junk food, start smoking, and score significantly lower on reading, math, and language arts exams. Keeping TV out of your child's bedroom is an easy, essential form of preventive medicine.

The same goes for other digital devices, like handhelds and gaming systems. Kids don't need the temptation and distraction of digital media—and instant access to it—at all hours of the day and night. By keeping media out of the bedroom, you can control it and prevent your child from developing health and academic problems and addictive habits. The best strategy is to keep digital media in common areas of your home and set firm time limits. Whether your child is watching a cartoon, playing Angry Birds on a smartphone, digital fingerpainting on an iPad, or playing a Wii game, it all counts.

It's also very important to have digital-media-free family time— at mealtimes, for example, and before bed—and to make sure that the TV isn't constantly on at home, so your child isn't surrounded by the conversation killing drone of shows and commercials.

It's equally important to minimize your own digital distraction. You might be tethered to your smartphone for work or planning purposes, but don't let it interrupt your time with your child. Turn off your phone, close your laptop, and switch off the TV when you spend time with your child. It's the best way to teach her that digital media is never more important than human connection. I can't emphasize the importance of role-modeling enough.

2. Teach your child that media use is a privilege, not a right.

If your five- or six-year-old wants to watch *Phineas and Ferb,* play Line Surfer on your iPhone, or play Nintendogs on the DS, now's the time to teach him to ask permission. It's an easy way to get him to start thinking that using digital media is a privilege, not an ever-present option that he's always entitled to. At this age, your child is learning to ask permission before he takes something out of the fridge, borrows a friend's toy, interrupts a grown-up, or goes into the backyard. Asking permission to use digital devices won't seem strange at all, and it's a great way to train him to see media use as a special, occasional treat and reward for his good behavior.

3. Stay involved. Use the Internet and watch TV with your child, limit exposure to age-inappropriate content, and be prepared to explain things she may see but not understand.

Even if you've installed a child-safe Web browser on your computer, it's still important to go on to the Internet with your five- or six-year-old, because chances are, she's going to see something that you wish she hadn't. Using the KidZui browser, for example, she can click on the Lovely Spring Dress Up game, where the first image she sees is a tall, thin girl with unnaturally long legs wearing bikini panties and a bra. Your child can dress her in a micro-mini and thigh-high black fishnets, or she can play the Flight Attendant Dress Up or Pretty Secretary Make-Up games, all featuring supermodel-thin female characters.

At this age, media can reinforce stereotypes and influence kids' expectations. If you're sitting beside your child while she's browsing and playing Internet games, you can balance what she sees with your own opinions about body image, positive female role models, and gender stereotypes. It's an important issue, because girls as young as five and six are already getting the message from media and peers that thin is beautiful and that there's something wrong with them if they don't look like the distorted body types they see on the screen. In one 2009 study, nearly half of all three- to six-year-old girls said they worried about getting fat.[11]

That's why it's so important, at this age, to use media *with* your child. At five and six, kids believe and imitate what they see. They can't distinguish between fact and fantasy, and they don't understand the difference between ads and regular media content. They need their parents to supervise, guide, and protect them from inappropriate material that's violent, scary, sexy, or filled with bad language, role models, and behavior.

If your child does see something that's inappropriate, use that moment as an opportunity to teach him something about your own values, what's real, what's make-believe, and what's important. Your five- or six-year-old is learning from everything he sees and does, and it's important that he learns the most essential lessons about life, values, and expectations from you.

4. Understand that marketers aggressively target children, and that kids this age are especially vulnerable, since they can't easily distinguish between fantasy and reality.
Five- and six-year-olds often don't know the difference between ads and regular media content, and they don't realize that advertisers are trying to get them to crave junk food, toys, and other things they're trying to sell. That's exactly what makes them such a desirable target for advertisers and so susceptible to marketing ploys.

Companies spend around $400 million a year on TV ads aimed at kids under twelve, pushing sugary, salty, high-fat, unhealthy food. Kids, on average, see fourteen of these ads a day, and that doesn't include hidden marketing schemes, like product placements on popular TV shows. Add to this marketing barrage the blizzard of pop-up and banner advertising on children's websites and the fact that branded sites, like TrixWorld and McDonald's HappyMeal.com, are filled with "advergames" entirely geared to promoting products, and you have a perfect storm when it comes to encouraging kids to crave junk food, sodas, and other unhealthy snacks. Childhood obesity rates are higher than ever, leading far too many kids to face an unhealthy future. And a big reason is because these ads are effective.

But food marketers aren't the only companies trying to profit off the lack of sophistication of little kids. Popular games like Smurf's Village feature in-app purchases that are wildly expensive traps. The goal of the game is to build a cozy village for the Smurfs to live in. You can make their hometown even nicer by making their gardens lush and loaded with berries. All it takes to make this happen is to go to the onscreen Smurfberry Shop and buy a bucket of Smurfberries for $4.99, or six wag-onloads for $99.99. Little kids have no idea that they're spending *actual money* for virtually nothing—and even older kids can rack up enormous bills on their parents' iTunes accounts. One Maryland eight-year-old, for example, charged $1,400 in Smurfberries on her mom's iPhone. This isn't an unusual ploy by game marketers. A five-year-old I know charged $250 to his grandfather on Wham-O's Frisbee Forever game by buying "star coins" to play with cool-looking digital discs that don't really exist. He had no idea what he had done, and his grandfather had no clue that he'd be stuck with a huge bill for a "free" game.

Marketers like these are exploiting the fact that kids and the grownups in their lives can be easy marks. To avoid the in-app money pits, don't tell your child your iTunes password, and change the settings on your device to restrict in-app purchases. It's just as important to steer your five- or six-year-old away from the persuasive influence of ads and marketing. Choose commercial-free TV shows, or use a DVR service that lets you skip the ads. Teach your child the difference between a commercial and a TV show and to spot the ads on TV, videos, games, and websites. You can make it a fun "advergame" so that your child learns to spot the marketing tricks before the ads trick him.

5. Be careful about what you post on social networks: don't give out your child's full name, address, and birth date; don't post birthday party information or tag photos; check your privacy settings; and make sure you're on a closed network.

Life is full of big moments for five- and six-year-olds, from the first day of kindergarten to Pee Wee Soccer practice, birthday parties, and teddy bear picnics. With smartphone cameras and social networks, it's easier than ever to capture and share all these moments with friends and family. But be careful. Technology is making it easier to share photographs, but it's also revealing a lot more than you think about the shots you post, including the location and exact time they were taken.

Most smartphones have a built-in GPS chip, and the phone camera captures that information and attaches it digitally to the picture. When you post the photo to the Internet, it's surprisingly easy for someone to access that information with a downloadable computer program. Of course, this data isn't of interest to most people you'd want to share the photo with. But there are others out there who could misuse it.

That's why it's important to use a photo-sharing site, like Flickr and Picasa, that lets you carefully restrict access to photos you post. It's also a good idea to turn off the geolocation services on your phone settings. Think twice before posting, since pictures of your child that you post on the Internet can become part of her permanent digital history. And never tag photos of children or add names, addresses, birth dates, or any other identifying information to photo captions. Think before you post and be careful when you share. That way, you'll keep private moments and personal information in the right hands.

Ages Seven to Eight

Seven- and eight-year-olds are beginning to taste freedoms and responsibility, from walking on their own to a neighbor's house to doing homework and helping out with chores at home. They've got stronger ties with peers, interests of their own, and a growing fascination with popular culture. As their abilities and confidence increase, it's up to parents to set firm boundaries, provide rules and guidance, and teach them how to be safe and healthy in their expanding world.

It's not just the real world that's bigger for kids at this age. They're also spending time exploring and inhabiting virtual worlds like Club Penguin and Poptropica. In these online, imaginary neighborhoods, they're creating virtual identities, furnishing virtual rooms, and making online friends with whom they can play and chat. They may also be buying virtual clothing, toys, and accessories—sometimes with *real money*. More than 8 million kids in the United States alone visit these sites on a regular basis, so it's an alternative reality that many parents of seven- and eight-year-olds have to deal with. That means keeping a watchful eye on what your kid's doing and where she's going in the *physical* world as well as in the *online* playgrounds and social circles she's inhabiting. Technology makes many things simpler, but raising a child in the digital age isn't one of them.

Gaming, too, is a dramatically bigger attraction for seven- and eight-year-olds,[1] but TV is the main draw.[2] Many kids this age—more than half[3]—have TVs in their own rooms, and those kids tend to spend more time watching television than other children. They're also exposed to more TV advertising for fast food as well as sugary and salty snacks, giving them a higher risk of obesity and related health problems. Kids are impressionable, and companies count on that. Marketers spend many millions of dollars a year targeting children, and it's very effective. A 2009 study by Yale University researchers showed that kids ages seven to eleven who watched a half-hour cartoon with food commercials ate 45 percent more snack food while they watched the show than kids who watched the same program *without* commercials.

Marketers are also reaching kids through websites like McWorld, sponsored by McDonald's, and Create a Comic, which is designed to sell Honey Nut Cheerios. At an age when kids are still naïve about advertising and wide-eyed about digital media, they're easy marks for companies that can reach them more directly and cheaply than ever through the Web. That's another reason for parents to keep a close eye on what their kids are doing online and offline, set firm media rules, and teach kids to be as safe and aware in the digital world as they are crossing the street.

The bottom line is that seven- and eight-year-olds are growing up amid an explosion of electronic devices, digital content, and media options. Screens are everywhere—in their pockets, at school, in their bedrooms, and in almost every area of the house. Without strict media rules, it's far too easy for kids to become heavy consumers. And research shows that heavy media users are more likely to get poor grades, get into trouble, and be bored and unhappy. Studies also show that kids who spend less time with media feel more content over all.

The good news is that parents can make a big difference. When they limit their kids' media use, their children spend less time in front of screens. They consume less media when they don't have a TV or other digital devices in their bedrooms, when the TV is off at mealtimes, and when parents set firm family media rules and stick to them. The digital media habits that your child forms now can make a huge and important difference in his life as he gets older.

This is the time to give your child rules and tools for navigating the virtual and physical worlds safely. The answers and tips below can help you do it.

What Parents Want to Know

1. Should I sign my kid up for a subscription to a virtual world?
Online virtual worlds like Club Penguin, Webkinz, Neopets, Poptropica, and Wonder Rotunda are hugely popular with kids, starting at age seven or eight. About half a billion kids under fifteen visit them regularly. But I would be very careful about letting your child spend time in these online communities, for several reasons.

These sites function as online arcades where kids can play games, adopt a pet, decorate a room or an igloo, and play with virtual friends. They can role play, explore cartoon geography, and roam these worlds independently, which is very appealing and fun for kids this age. That doesn't mean, however, that you should allow your child to wander around virtual communities unsupervised.

Most of the sites claim they're safe environments for kids, and they feature parental controls, monitored chat rooms, and rules for online behavior. But kids, especially older players, can figure out how to get around the rules, and your child can be exposed to bad language, bullying, and inappropriate virtual behavior. Because players are anonymous—assuming cartoony alter egos called "avatars"—some may say things and misbehave in ways they wouldn't in a real environment.

Many of the virtual worlds also tout their creative and educational value. It's true that your child can have fun designing and accessorizing her own avatar and online living environment, but the main lesson many of these sites teach is consumerism. Some virtual playgrounds—like McWorld and Trix World, sponsored by General Mills—are blatant marketing gambits designed to get kids to associate their products with fun and games.[4] And all these sites exist primarily to make money. Some do it by charging subscriptions; others are loaded with ads, and many focus mainly on encouraging kids to spend real money to purchase imaginary items like "smurfberries" and accessories for their avatars and igloos. These sites can get expensive to visit, and many promote consumerism more than anything else. They can also be addicting. They're entertaining and engrossing and can easily suck up way too much of your child's time.

I'd also think twice before launching your child into an online social networking environment at the age of seven or eight. These virtual neighborhoods may be more kid-friendly than Facebook, but they immerse your child in the two-dimensional world of digital companionship. That's part of the reality they're growing up in, but in my view, it's better to keep them focused on real-world friends and relationships as long as possible.

If you do want to let your child explore a virtual world, here's what I'd recommend:

- **Explore the site.** Try it out for yourself by creating your own avatar and see what the site's virtual neighborhoods, shops, and inhabitants are really like. Then decide if it's a place where you think your child should be spending time.
- **Make it safe.** Set parental controls and scripted chat settings and don't let your child wander around by herself. Know where she is, where she's going, and what she's doing at all times, just as you would in the real world.
- **Show and tell.** Teach your child how to be safe and behave appropriately online. Make sure he knows that he should never share personal information or passwords online, and that he should never say something in a virtual world that he wouldn't say to someone's face in real life.
- **Talk to your child about money.** These sites can be expensive and very materialistic, so talk about your values and concerns.
- **Set time limits.** Use an alarm clock or kitchen timer to make it very clear when it's time for your child to get off the com-

puter. And make sure that the time she spends online is part of her two-hour-a-day maximum in front of a screen.

2. Should I let my kid play online games?

At age seven and eight, kids are increasingly attracted to interactive media. Most of them are playing digital games on a handheld device, Nintendo DS, Xbox, Wii, PlayStation, or other consoles.[5] Many kids also like to go to free sites—like Game Wing, PopCap Games, and GirlsGo-Games—that offer lots of different online activities, from sports, puzzles, and word games to pet care, dress-up, cooking, quizzes, and arcade games. Because they're online, your child can play them on a computer, smartphone, iPad, and any device that has Internet access.

Some of these portals feature only prescreened games that are okay for kids this age, but others include first-person shooter games and others that are inappropriate for seven- and eight-year-olds. Many free gaming portals are also filled with ads and marketing contests, while others, like luckycharms.com, are outright product promotions designed to reach and cultivate young consumers. Some portals for girls reinforce traditional gender notions—for example, that girls should only focus on cooking, fashion, makeup, and flirting with boys.

So I'd be very careful and selective about online games. Check out the reviews, ratings, and recommendations and play them yourself before you let your seven- or eight-year-old spend time on them. And make sure that time is limited. Many portals boast that they have "addicting" games, and that's no exaggeration. Research shows that digital game playing triggers the release of dopamine, a chemical that stimulates the pleasure and reward circuits of the brain, like addictive drugs. The more kids play, the more likely they are to get hooked on gaming—and digital game addiction is linked to depression as well as social and school problems.

So set clear time limits on gaming. Be firm about them, and keep your child away from violent games, because studies link them to aggressive behavior and lack of empathy. Make sure your child plays online games where you can see and supervise them. Don't let him play games before bed, since digital excitement and stimulation can cause sleep problems. And say no to online multiplayer games where your child can compete and chat with friends or strangers on the Internet. At seven or eight, your child needs to focus on learning face-to-face social skills in the real world.

3. How should I handle digital media issues on playdates?

Think of it this way: if your child had an allergy to peanuts or strawberries, you would certainly tell the parent of any child who invited her over for a playdate. Digital media rules are no different from food rules. You know what's good for your seven- or eight-year-old and what's not, and it's important to share that information with anyone who's supervising your child, whether that's a relative, babysitter, or a friend's parent. So whether the issue is screen time, scary movies, or gaming rules, make sure you speak up. You can't control everything your child is exposed to as her world gets bigger, but you can definitely increase your influence and comfort level by communicating openly.

4. Should I get net-minder software?

Kids love to explore in real life and online, and chances are your seven- or eight-year-old is no stranger to searching on the Internet to find out what's there. Unfortunately, it's all too easy for your child to stumble upon content that you wish he hadn't seen by typing innocent words and phrases into a search box.

Still, there are many things you can do to reduce, if not eliminate, unintended encounters. First, make sure your child uses the computer and other devices that have Web access in a common area, where you can supervise and guide his online activity. Second, set up parental controls and Internet content filters on your Web browsers, including Internet Explorer, Firefox, and Safari, as well as search engines like Google, Yahoo!, and Bing. Internet content filters block inappropriate sites that are linked to key words. Although some sites may slip through these filters, they provide a basic level of protection and peace of mind.

To take Web filtering another step, make sure your seven- or eight-year-old uses a child-friendly Web browser like KidZui, which will connect him only to sites that are prescreened and safe. You can also install net-minder software programs that let you customize filter levels for each family member and track your child's online activity.

And don't forget to set parental controls on the Wii, Nintendo DS, iPad, smartphones, and other devices that connect to the Web. You can also restrict the kind of content your child is able to download from iTunes. Check out www.commonsense.org for specific suggestions, instructions, and recommendations for controls and filters.

These protection features are helpful and important, but they're not foolproof. The best way to make sure your child doesn't see things she shouldn't on the Web is to search with her on the Internet and make sure you know what she's doing and discovering online.

5. Is it okay for my child to watch YouTube?

Kids love YouTube; it's been their number-one Internet search term.[6] On YouTube they can find episodes of their favorite TV programs, popular music videos, and silly or inspiring clips posted by other kids. But they can also come across postings with mature content and rude and crude viewer comments on even age-appropriate videos.

The bottom line is that YouTube is not meant for kids under thirteen. Seven- to eight-year-olds should not be exploring it on their own. They may be watching something perfectly innocent, but the list of suggested videos that pops up may include clips that are wildly inappropriate, and it's too easy for kids to click on the links and see things you wouldn't want them to.

A good idea is to make sure your child only goes on YouTube through a kid-friendly browser like KidZui, which will let her see only prescreened, age-appropriate postings. Otherwise, if your seven- or eight-year-old wants to watch a YouTube video, watch it with him. You should also check the Safety Mode box at the bottom of each YouTube page to filter suggestions and search results. Inappropriate clips, however, can still slip through the filter, so it's always important to keep a close eye on what your kid is watching.

What Parents Need to Know

1. Embrace your child's digital world and understand it.

If children are digital natives, parents are immigrants—struggling to learn the vocabulary, norms, and reality of kids' digital lives. It's definitely a tough job. Technology changes at a head-spinning pace, and what we grew up with has little to do with our kids' experience. From Webkinz and Club Penguin to Wii Bowling and Angry Birds, they're seeing and playing things we never dreamed of in our own youth. As busy as we are, it's often hard to make time to play their games, explore sites they're visiting, and familiarize ourselves with their digital worlds.

But it's crucial to do that. If we don't know what our kids are doing and where they're going when they're online, it's hard to know what the risks are and how to keep them healthy and safe.

So take the time to explore your child's digital playgrounds. Create an avatar and experience the virtual world that he likes to spend time in. Play We Ski and Cut the Rope so you can understand the fun he has with those games and apps and keep them from being isolating, solitary activities. Find a YouTube video your child will love and show it to him. Watch the TV shows she watches, decide which ones you think are okay, and record them on a digital video recorder so you can skip the ads. Knowledge is power. When you know what your child is doing in the digital world, you can take control.

2. Discuss appropriate online behaviors and family and website rules for using the Internet.

This is the perfect age to start teaching your child about responsible online behavior and safety. If she's exploring virtual worlds, which are like social networks for younger kids, or playing games online, she needs to know important online dos and don'ts:

- **Explain your family's rules.** Let her know which sites are okay for her to go on and which aren't. And make it clear that she's got strict time limits when she goes online, that you need to supervise what she is doing, and that the computer or gaming device goes off when her time is up.

- **Explain the website's rules.** Kids' Internet sites, like Club Penguin and Dizzywood, post rules of behavior. Go online with your child and make sure he understands them before he begins playing. Explain that kids who break the rules can lose their playing privileges.

- **Teach your child that the rules for online and real-life behavior are exactly the same.** You have to play nicely, you can't act like a bully, and you should never say or do something to others that you wouldn't want someone to say or do to you.

- **Tell your child to let you know if anyone acts mean or does something inappropriate on the site.** Many websites have tools that let you report online misbehavior. Show your child how she can use them.

- **Help your kid understand that not everything he sees online is true**—and that not everyone he meets online is who they say they are.

Like any privilege, going online comes with responsibilities. By teaching your seven- or eight-year-old how to behave and be safe online, you're laying the groundwork for positive digital experiences and relationships as he gets older.

3. Teach your child not to share personal information or passwords online.

If your child is starting to go online—to explore Club Penguin, for example, or to play on gaming portals—it's not too early for her to learn about online safety. Go online with your seven- or eight-year-old when she sets up an account. Help her make up a screen name that doesn't give away her real identity. Next, help her think up a password that nobody can guess, not even her brother or her best friend. To be safe, she should never use her nickname, a pet's name, her birth date, the family's address or phone number, or any other kind of personal information that people may know. The best passwords use letters, numbers, and made-up words that you can't find in a dictionary, and they can be fun to create. Making a game of it is a great way to teach your child the basics of password safety. Explain that she should never tell her password to anybody, not even a friend.

Before your seven- or eight-year-old goes online, also make sure that he knows he should never share personal information—his name, address, phone number, age, school, after-school activities, or anyone's e-mail address—with any people or avatars he may meet on the Web. When people use online identities, it's like they're wearing masks, and they're not always who they appear to be. He would never give that information to strangers in real life, and people on the Internet are strangers, too.

Another good rule is to tell your child never to download anything without asking you first. A lot of tantalizing, free, downloadable Internet games and videos are Trojan horses filled with malicious viruses and spyware that can infect your computer. And here's an important money-saving safety tip: don't let your child know and use your iTunes password. That way, she won't be able to download apps or make expensive in-app purchases, like virtual Frisbees and smurfberries, without your permission.

Teaching your child Internet safety basics at this age is as important as teaching her not to talk to strangers or to look both ways before crossing the street. Children today are growing up in two worlds—physical and virtual—and it's up to parents to teach them how to stay safe and healthy in *both*.

4. Start a family media diet and get the whole family involved in planning it.

Digital media is a lot like junk food. In small quantities, it's okay, but consuming too much of it on a daily basis just isn't healthy. That's why parents don't let their kids eat whatever they want whenever they want it. What kids put in their bodies affects their health, how they perform in school, and their well-being.

Digital media is no different. It's like junk food or dessert—a small serving is enough. The main courses in your child's day should be physical and creative activity, homework, and real-life, face-to-face interaction with friends and family. Digital media should be a treat, but for far too many kids, it's the main event. Many seven- and eight-year-olds spend more hours a day watching a screen than they do in school or with their families. It's like they're eating more junk food than anything else. The result, long term, is a greater risk of obesity and related illnesses, as well as academic, attention, behavior, and relationship problems.

So just as you control what your child eats, you need to manage her media diet. Many experts, including the American Academy of Pediatrics (AAP), recommend that you start a family media diet and stick to it. It's a project you can all do together.

The first step is for each member of the family to keep a media diary for a week, writing down each time they use media and for how long. You'll all quickly become a lot more conscious of the media you're using and how much time you're spending with it.

The next step is to come up with a healthy media diet for your family, with clear limits on the total number of hours each member can spend in front of a screen. For kids, the AAP recommends no more than two hours a day, and I'd personally recommend a lower limit. You might want to make exceptions for occasional "splurges," like the Super Bowl or a long family movie you want to watch together. But it's a good idea to keep all media off at mealtimes and before bed, out of your child's room, and in a common area.

Your seven- or eight-year-old may decide to spend part of his media time playing with an iPad, watching a cartoon, or browsing on Webkinz. But just as he shouldn't help himself to ice cream and cookies before asking you, make sure he always asks permission before using a digital device or watching TV. As his parent, it's important for you to be the gatekeeper, to know what he's doing, playing, and watching, when, and for how long.

That also means steering your kid toward media with positive role models and messages and away from shows, movies, games, and websites that include nudity or simulated sex. You should also be on the lookout for smoking, alcohol, or drug use; a lot of profanity; and any violence, aggression, or bullying that's used to resolve conflict and doesn't show instant consequences. The media normalizes behavior, and it's up to you to set the acceptable standards for your own family.

5. Lead by example—be a role model.

It's hard to encourage your seven- or eight-year-old not to eat junk food if you're always reaching for candy bars and bags of chips. It's the same when it comes to digital media. You have to teach by example.

If you keep the TV on during meals, check your e-mails when your child's trying to talk to you, or text a friend while she's trying to show you what she made at school, you're teaching her that technology is more important than she is. If you're looking at a screen instead of making eye contact, or emotional contact, with your child, you're sending the message that digital media is more important than human relationships. In short, you're modeling behavior that she'll mimic as she grows up.

The only way you can control your child's media consumption is by controlling yours first. If you want your child to lead a balanced life that's not tethered to digital screens, make sure you unplug, turn off your cell phone or your laptop, and turn off the TV during family time. Your child learns more from watching you than from what you say. So show him that you control your digital media and that it's never a distraction that keeps you from connecting with him.

Ages Nine to Ten

Nine- and ten-year-olds are tuned in to media stars, music, edgy content and language. Many also love online gaming, downloading, and hanging out with their peers. Impressionable and aware, on the threshold of adolescence, they're immersed in a culture that's dictated and defined by digital media.

Almost all of them—more than 90 percent of boys and girls—are playing games online.[1] Combat games are a big deal for boys, and some are bugging their parents to buy violent T-rated (teen) and M-rated (mature) video games like Grand Theft Auto and Call of Duty: Black Ops. Hold your ground and say no! When kids spend a lot of time playing games with participatory violence—massacring virtual opponents with guns and chain saws—they're more likely to have aggressive behavior, anxiety, and a lack of empathy. Instead, steer your child to great age-appropriate video games, like Guitar Hero or Wii Sports Resort, that strengthen motor skills rather than "kill skills" and that the whole family can play together.

Pay attention, too, to Web portals like GirlsGoGames that focus almost exclusively on makeup, flirting, and fashion. At an age when girls are forming their own identities, these sites intensify rampant media pressure on them to be "hot," conventional, and constantly focused on their appearance. Other online portals like Miss O & Friends and video games like The Daring Game for Girls are better choices for nine- and ten-year-olds who are looking for role models and exploring female identity. Gaming, however, can become a huge time waster for both girls and boys this age, so make sure you set firm media rules about time and content.

That's equally true when it comes to videos and TV. Most nine- and ten-year-olds have televisions in their bedrooms, which makes it especially difficult to control what and when they're watching.[2] Most are still watching age-appropriate shows like *Jonas, iCarly,* and *The Wizards of Waverly Place,* but they're also moving on from the Disney Channel and Nickelodeon to MTV, reality shows, and other adult-oriented prime-time programming. It may seem harmless to let your child watch popular shows like *Glee* and *Gossip Girl,* but they're full of sexual themes and content that can distort your child's understanding and expectations. A 2010 study by the American Academy of Pediatrics (AAP) found that 75 percent of prime-time programs contain sexual content and talk about sex as often as eight to ten times an hour, but they rarely mention the risks and responsibilities of sex. At nine and ten, your child is years away from being sexually active, but what he or she sees now, the AAP says, can influence the timing and impact of that experience. Kids who have TVs in their rooms are more likely than others to engage in early, risky sexual activity.

When it comes to movies, sexual content, violence, profanity, and gore are also big issues at this age. At nine and ten, kids often start lobbying parents to see PG-13 movies, many of which are promoted with marketing campaigns targeted to kids and previews "approved for all audiences." Any parent of a child this age who has squirmed through *Planet of the Apes* or *Transformers: Dark of the Moon* knows how edgy PG-13 movies can be. But you're in control. Your child might be eager to "age up" to more mature movies, but limiting exposure to age-appropriate content in all media is a smart move. Nine- and ten-year-olds want to fit in with their peers. And media, as the AAP states, is a "super peer" that can make kids believe that violence, profanity, smoking, drinking, drug use, and risky sexual activity are normal behavior.

Those messages are reinforced in a lot of music that kids this age listen to. According to a study in 2011, many of the songs getting top airplay include profanity or references to sex, drugs, or alcohol.[3] So change the radio station or listen to an age-appropriate playlist or CD and talk to your child about any lyrics that you find objectionable. You can't filter out every inappropriate media exposure in your child's life, but you can make sure that he hears your words in his head the next time he listens to a raunchy song.

The fact is, at nine and ten, you've got a lot of influence. Your child is paying attention to what his peers are doing—that's why he may suddenly be asking for a cell phone or T-rated video game. But you're the decision maker when it comes to your kid's media life, and the following answers and tips can help you make the best calls.

What Parents Want to Know

1. Should I get my kid a cell phone?

No, not yet! My personal view is that kids shouldn't have cell phones until they're ready for high school, for a lot of reasons. The most important point to keep in mind is that most cell phones these days are "smart." They're not just phones—they're powerful, pocket-size, highly addictive devices that kids can use for going online, downloading, taking photos and videos, texting, playing games, and endlessly distracting themselves when they should be paying attention at home, at school, or to other people. Giving your child a smartphone at nine or ten encourages her to be tethered to a digital screen instead of focusing on real people and the world around her. It's also putting powerful communication technology in her hands before she has the judgment and maturity to use it wisely. It's way too easy to take an embarrassing photo or video and share it with the world without thinking of the consequences. Your child could send or receive inappropriate text messages, play massively multiplayer online games, and communicate with anybody privately, out of your sight and with no supervision.

Money is an issue, too. Smartphones aren't cheap, and until your child is responsible enough not to lose it, drop it, or treat it like a toy, it's a risky investment. Cell phone bills, too, can be a shock if your kid exceeds texting and time limits and downloads expensive apps and ringtones.

But the biggest cost might be the addiction and distraction of a powerful digital communication and gaming device in your child's pocket. The last thing most nine- or ten-year-olds need is a digital screen that's always at their disposal, without supervision. One of the most challenging skills kids need to learn, in the digital age, is how to focus. And the constant temptation of texting and gaming can keep them from developing the ability to concentrate on one task at a time, whether it's a homework assignment or a conversation. According to a 2010 study by Stanford communications professor Clifford Nass, cell phone ownership at this age is linked to media multitasking. His study also showed that when girls this age multitask, they feel less socially successful and more pressure from peers.

So my advice is delay, delay, delay. Your kid might bug you for a phone, saying all her friends have them, but less than a third of nine- and ten-year-olds actually do. By saying no now, you're giving her time to stay focused on face-to-face communication and the real world around her instead of tethering her attention to a glowing screen.

2. What digital games are okay for my kid to play?

Almost all nine- and ten-year-olds play digital games on computers, game consoles, and handheld devices. Gaming is a huge preoccupation for preteens. According to a 2010 study, more than 90 percent of girls and boys between ages eight and eleven play online games, many of them on free sites like MiniClip, GirlsGoGames,[4] and Addictinggames.com or on virtual worlds like Club Penguin and Webkinz. Kids this age, especially boys, also start wanting to play T- or M-rated video games like Gears of War and Call of Duty: Modern Warfare.

Your answer, experts say, should be "absolutely no." T-rated games (teens, age 13+) often contain violent content, crude language, and suggestive themes, while M-rated games (mature, age 17+) are often ultra-violent and contain graphic sexual scenes and sexual violence. Study after study shows that kids who are repeatedly exposed to these games become inured to violence and less able to empathize. According to the American Academy of Pediatrics, violent electronic games are also directly linked to anxiety, bullying, and aggressive behavior. For kids this age, *no* game that involves blood, first-person shooting, or sexual violence is appropriate in any way, and any depiction of violence in games should show consequences and the resulting pain and suffering instead of triumph.

So the first rule of thumb is to *pay attention to the ratings* on video game boxes. The only games appropriate for your nine- or ten-year-old are those that are rated E (everyone, ages 6+). But even those can contain some violence and crude language. So the second rule is to *know the content of the games before you let your child play them.* This is especially important with online games and downloadable gaming apps, which are often free and have no ratings or age restrictions. Any kid can easily access them and start playing if parents aren't paying attention. Casual gaming sites like Addictinggames.com can have disgustingly violent first-person shooter games, and Apple's iTunes app store has free, downloadable hack-and-slash bloodfests like Samurai: Vengeance. So play the game yourself before you let your child play it, and keep in mind that many games get much bloodier when you get to higher levels.

The same goes for online games targeted to girls. Many games on casual sites like GirlsGames1 reinforce gender stereotypes, focusing on flirting, kissing, fashion, and makeup, and some encourage poor choices and bad behavior. CheatMasters, for example, challenges players to win points by peeking at other students' papers in a virtual classroom. Media teaches by example, both positive and negative, so prescreen your child's games to make sure they're teaching the right message.

There are, however, plenty of great options that can keep your child's gaming time fun and productive. Here are some tips for finding the best games for your nine- or ten-year-old:

- Look for games related to your child's interests, whether that's sports, strategy, music, or fantasy. Get suggestions from other parents, and check out ratings and recommendations at www.commonsense.org.

- Choose nonviolent games that are exciting and challenging.
- Pick games that build your kid's strategy and problem-solving skills.
- Find games, especially active ones, that friends and family members can play to make gaming a social instead of an isolating activity.
- As I've said before, set firm time limits and stick to them. Any time your child spends playing digital games should be part of his two hours a day *total* in front of a screen.
- Balance your child's digital gaming with physical games like soccer and softball, reading, and unstructured time to think, dream, and see where his own imagination takes him.

3. How can I enforce my family's media rules when my kid is spending a lot of time at his friends' houses?
As kids get more independent, it becomes more difficult to control the media they're consuming. And it's very likely that when your nine- or ten-year-old is spending time at his friends' houses, he's spending at least part of that time sitting in front of a screen.

But there are two things you can do to increase the chances that he'll stick to your family's media rules when he's away from home. Think of it like this: if your child had a food allergy, you'd make sure he understood the rules about what he can eat and the consequences if he didn't follow them. You'd also make sure to communicate those rules to the parent of any friend he was spending time with.

The same strategy applies when it comes to media. First, make sure your child understands the family media rules. Reinforce them clearly and often and explain what the consequences will be if your child breaks them. Second, speak up about those rules, in advance, to the parents of any friends with whom your child is spending time. Between their supervision and your child's understanding of rules and consequences, there's a good chance you'll minimize his exposure to media that's out of bounds.

As kids get older, they make more decisions on their own. They don't live in a bubble, and they learn how to make good choices through experience and occasional mistakes. As a parent, you can reward the good decisions and enforce the consequences of bad ones. You can also mitigate the effects of inappropriate media exposure—if your child plays an M-rated video game, for example, or watches a movie with adult content at a friend's house—by discussing it with him and sharing your values and point of view. Your child will remember those words when you aren't with him, and they'll help him make better, healthier decisions for himself.

4. How can I manage and supervise my kid's escalating media use?

There's no question that at nine and ten, kids consume more media than ever. They're surrounded by screens on TVs, computers, game consoles, handhelds, and smartphones. And more of them are starting to use several devices at once, multitasking in ways that can be hard to manage.

But it's essential to limit and supervise your child's screen time. According to a 2010 study, the more time preteens spend in front of a screen, the more likely they are to feel sad, lonely, and negative, no matter how much physical activity they get.[5] When kids have prolonged exposure to violent media content, they're more likely to become anxious and desensitized to violence and behave aggressively. And regular exposure to sexualized media content increases the odds that kids will have earlier and riskier sexual experiences.

Consuming media is too often a sedentary, isolating activity. By age nine and ten, most kids are spending more than five hours a day in front of a screen—despite the fact that the American Academy of Pediatrics advises a total of no more than two hours a day. The good news, however, is that when parents make an effort to curb their media use, kids spend less time in front of a screen. And children who spend less time gaping at screens are more content and more likely to do well in school.

Here are some simple ways in which you can manage and supervise your child's media use and keep it within healthy bounds:

- Set firm limits on how much media your child consumes— no more than two hours a day, total, in front of any kind of screen. If you need to, use a kitchen timer to enforce the rules.
- Set clear limits on the kinds of media content. Your nine- or ten-year-old should stay away from media with sexual content, violence with no consequences, bad role models, smoking, and alcohol and drug use.
- Minimize media distraction and multitasking. Help your child focus on one thing at a time.
- Stay connected to your child's media world and know what he's playing, watching, and doing at home and at friends' houses.
- Encourage your kid to play active games—even better, to go out and play.
- Tape your child's favorite age-appropriate TV shows on a digital video recorder so she can skip the ads.
- Schedule regular media-free time—before homework, for example, at all meals, and before bed.
- Be a role model. Set a good example for your nine- or ten-year-old by minimizing your own media use, reading, being physically active, and leading a life that's balanced instead of media-focused.

5. My kid loves YouTube. Should I have concerns about that?

There are some great things about YouTube and others you should be cautious about. Its content, for example, cuts both ways. There are silly, hilarious, and inspiring videos that nine- or ten-year-olds love. In fact, YouTube is the top online video destination for kids age eleven and under. Your child can learn how to play guitar, do yoga, solve a Rubik's Cube puzzle, and make an omelet by watching YouTube videos.

But there's also a lot of obscenity, violence, and other inappropriate content on YouTube that's easy for kids to find accidentally. Your child might be watching a perfectly harmless video of dancing hamsters, and the suggested postings that pop up could include innocent-sounding links to X-rated material. The comments on kid-friendly videos can also be crude, cruel, and obscene.

The bottom line is that YouTube is not a site that kids should be exploring on their own. Membership on the site is restricted to those thirteen and up, and it attempts to flag or delete inappropriate content. But younger kids can fake their age to get a YouTube account, and even if you set account preferences to block flagged content, inappropriate material may still slip through. That's why your kid should do YouTube searches on a children's Web portal like KidZui that will only connect him to age-appropriate videos. Otherwise, you should prescreen any YouTube video your child wants to watch, keep the computer in a common area, and monitor what she's doing on the site.

Posting on YouTube is another issue to be concerned about. Any child this age with access to an advanced smartphone has the ability to video herself and post the clip on YouTube—without the judgment and sophistication to understand that it will be seen by a huge, invisible online audience including creeps and predators. One ten-year-old boy in Indiana posted a nude video of himself on YouTube because some teenage girls he met online asked him to. It turns out those teenagers were actually child predators preying on a little boy. Kids are naïve and very vulnerable to this kind of ruse.

They're also influenced by a youth media culture that glamorizes celebrity. A 2011 study by researchers at UCLA found that, for kids ages nine to eleven, fame is now the number-one trait they value, up from fifteenth place in 1997. At the same time, the importance of being kind to others fell to twelfth place, down from second in 1997. In a world where kids can fake their ages or get their parents to set up YouTube accounts, it can be tempting for them to post clips and video blogs ("vlogs") that can go viral and attract fifty thousand or a million hits. In no time, kids who aren't even supposed to be posting on the site can become YouTube "microfamous"—or, as one tween vlogger put it, more famous than the mayors of most small cities in the United States.

A handful of preteens, including gifted young singers, have launched themselves into the digital and even professional limelight through You-

Tube. But others can attract comments that may make them feel hated and stigmatized instead of popular or famous. That kind of experience can be devastating to deal with at an age when kids are just forming their own fragile identities.

So keep a close eye on your child when it comes to YouTube and make clear that posting her own videos is out of bounds. Kids may all want to be stars, as a TV producer said, but instant online attention can take dangerous turns.

What Parents Need to Know

1. If you decide to get your kid a cell phone, here's what to keep in mind.

My best advice is to put off giving your child a cell phone for as long as possible—ideally, until she's ready for high school. I recognize that in some family situations it makes sense to give a nine- or ten-year-old a phone for safety reasons. She may be going to and from school alone, for example, or spending other time unsupervised and out of sight of responsible adults. In those cases, a mobile phone can be an important lifeline and a tool for regularly communicating and checking in.

What your child needs in that situation is a phone, not a mobile computer, camera, gaming, and downloading device. The good news is that there are basic, inexpensive, prepaid cell phones on the market that don't come with unlimited texting; fancy, distracting features; and big bills for minutes and data plans. With a basic cell phone, which you can program with all the phone numbers your child needs, you can have the security of voice communication without adding to your child's digital distractions. If you keep things simple with a stripped-down starter phone, you can teach your child the basics of cell phone safety and responsibility:

- Never answer a call from a phone number you don't know.
- Don't lose your phone.

- Charge it every night.
- Turn it off in class, at the dinner table, and before bedtime.

With a simple "cell phone with training wheels," your child can stay in safe contact with you and start preparing for the privilege of having a more powerful smartphone when she gets older.

2. If you haven't already set family media rules, do it now, before the teen years.
At age nine or ten, your child still looks to you for guidance and permission. You're the biggest influence in his life, so if you haven't done so already, now's the time to set family media rules, when they can still have a major impact on his habits and choices.

Here's what I'd recommend:

- Go over Internet safety rules, reminding your child never to share any personal information or respond to strangers on the Web and to treat others with respect when she's online.
- Keep TV and all digital devices out of your child's bedroom.
- Set parental controls on the TV, computer, handhelds, gaming consoles, and smartphones.
- Remind your child to ask permission before using any digital media.
- Agree on regular media-free times—during meals and homework, for example, and before bed.
- Make a rule that your child needs to read, exercise, or play every day for at least the same amount of time that he spends using media.
- Discuss the consequences if your kid breaks the rules—for example, spending a weekend with no digital media.
- Explain the rules to other family members, babysitters, and the parents of friends your child spends time with.

- Use media with your child as much as possible; know what your child is watching and listening to; and share your values.
- Be a role model. Set a good media example by turning off the TV and computer, putting away your cell phone, and spending uninterrupted face-to-face time with your child.

3. Do your homework—look at the websites, movies, games, and other digital media that your child is interested in before she does.

You can't manage your child's media life if you don't know what she's watching, playing, and listening to. So put in the time and explore her digital world. Start by asking her what she likes to do online, what digital games she likes to play, what movies and TV shows she likes to watch, and what music she listens to. Ask her to show you the sites and games that she spends time on. Ask her to play you her favorite songs and tell you why she likes them. Say what you think, too, without being judgmental; chances are, she'll appreciate that you take an interest.

Once you know what your child is doing with digital media, find out what her friends are doing and what else she's interested in. Then check out those games, movies, websites, and music. Experience them firsthand and read reviews and recommendations to decide whether they're appropriate for your kid. If not, tell your child and explain why. If he knows you're paying attention to his digital life, he'll pay closer attention to, and respect, what you have to say about it.

4. Seek out positive media experiences for your child.

No parent wants to say no all the time. So come up with some positive, age-appropriate digital experiences that your nine- or ten-year-old will enjoy. You can start by getting recommendations at www.commonsense. org. Check out the movies, programs, games, or websites yourself to make sure they're good fits for your child. Then keep a list of great media suggestions that are stimulating, fun, educational, and challenging. And encourage your kid to read! If he hasn't started the Harry Potter series, for example, now's the time.

5. Impart your values.

At nine or ten, your child is starting to spend more time out of your sight. He's increasingly relying on his own judgment and ability to handle challenges like peer pressure and his natural impulses to "age up."

The best way to prepare him to make good choices when you aren't around is to make sure he knows and understands your values. You might not be there when a friend asks him if he wants to play an M-rated video game like Mortal Kombat, but if you've shared your feelings with him about violent games, he'll hear your voice in his own head before he says yes or no. When you impart your values, your child will develop an inner compass that can point him in the right direction even when you're not there to guide him.

Ages Eleven to Twelve

On the brink of the teen years, eleven- and twelve-year-olds are emotional, impatient to grow up, and focused on their friends and fitting in. Their identities are taking shape while their bodies are changing. They're self-conscious and vulnerable to rejection, and they need plenty of guidance.

In the midst of change, they're learning how to manage peer relationships in the real world. They're also experimenting with virtual identities and friendships. By now, they're communicating with peers online as much as or more than they are face-to-face—instant messaging, texting if they have a cell phone, and Facebooking if they've set up an account, even though the site is legally restricted to users thirteen and up.

In their real and virtual social worlds, eleven- and twelve-year-olds are fragile and anxious. They're learning socially accepted norms, but they don't yet have the judgment to be safe, savvy, responsible, and self-protective in all situations. They're encountering lots of stuff, like Internet porn, that is very inappropriate and can distort their understanding of intimacy and relationships. And online interactions can be very intense. Given the viral nature of the Internet, tweens' lack of impulse control, and their ability to post instant images and anonymous comments, it's easy to see how situations can get cruelly or embarrassingly out of control—damaging feelings, friendships, and reputations.

As a parent of three teenagers, I know it's no longer possible to monitor everything your eleven- or twelve-year-old sees and does. That's why it's more important than ever to teach your tween responsible behavior, online and offline, share your values, and set clear rules and boundaries. Kids this age need the tools and time to learn how to be safe and smart as they become more independent and explore on their own. These answers and tips can help you guide your tween through both the perils and opportunities of the digital world.

What Parents Want to Know

1. Is it okay for my kid to watch PG-13 movies?

Movies rated for kids thirteen and up actively target younger kids through merchandising, previews dubbed "appropriate for all ages," and ads on TV channels like Cartoon Network and Nickelodeon. But that doesn't mean they're okay for your preteen to watch.

A PG-13 rating means "Parents Strongly Cautioned," and that's a warning you should take seriously. These movies have more violence, sexuality, nudity, and profanity than films rated PG (Parental Guidance Suggested), and they've been getting cruder, more explicit, and more violent over the years. Some are much too violent and sexually graphic for most eleven- and twelve-year-olds. Other PG-13 films, however, like *Harry Potter and the Deathly Hallows,* could be fine for a tween to see along with a parent, who can discuss any questionable scenes afterward.

The key is to find out as much as you can about the movie before deciding. Read reviews, talk to other parents, see the film yourself if you're not sure, and answer these questions before you make up your mind:

- **If the film has violence, does it show the consequences of pain and suffering?** Kids this age should not see movies

156

where violent behavior is rewarded or that have scenes of gratuitous, realistic brutality or horror.

- **Does the movie have adult sex scenes or show risky sexual behavior without consequences?** Simple kisses and boy/girl social dynamics are fine for kids to see at this age, but risky or advanced sexual activity is out of bounds.
- **Does it have scenes of drug and alcohol use or abuse?** Unless the movie shows clear consequences, it's not appropriate.
- **Does it glamorize smoking?** Be careful. According to the American Cancer Society, kids who see a lot of smoking in movies are about three times more likely to start smoking than other kids.

Bottom line, nobody knows your kid better than you do. If you decide that it's okay for your eleven- or twelve-year-old to see a PG-13 movie, watch it together. If it's on a DVD, you can skip over any scenes you think are inappropriate. And after you watch the film, use it as a "teachable moment." Talk about bad choices that characters make and have a conversation about behavior, consequences, and your own values. Bad examples are great opportunities to talk about safety issues, right and wrong, and responsibility.

2. Should I be concerned about how much my kid is instant messaging?

Electronic chatting through instant messaging (IMing) takes off at this age. Eleven- and twelve-year-olds are focused on their peers, and real-time, computer chatting on Gchat, iChat, AOL's AIM, and other instant messaging programs keeps them connected to their friends even when they're sitting at the family computer doing homework.

That's the problem. A kid who's instant messaging has a buddy list open on the computer screen that shows who's available to chat. Messages shoot back and forth, demanding instant responses, making it impossible for her to really focus on anything else. Many computers also have webcams, allowing real-time video chatting that takes digital distraction to another level. And distraction is a big reason to be concerned about IMing. When kids post messages while they're doing homework, their assignments take a lot longer to complete. And according to the National Academy of Sciences, they understand and retain less information when they study and instant message at the same time.

It can also become a compulsive habit. Kids can spend, or waste, literally hours IMing and video chatting with buddies. Every time a new message appears on the screen, they get a jolt of adrenaline. The message, no matter how inane or mundane, grabs their attention. And they're not always harmless chats. Forty percent of kids who've been cyberbullied say that it happened when they were instant messaging.[1] Studies show that kids also feel more peer pressure when they're communicating with friends online.[2] IMing can also be a problem if kids don't personally know everyone on their buddy lists, like "friends of friends" that nobody has ever met.

Here are some simple but important tips to help keep IMing under control:

- **Set time limits.** Any time your child spends IMing should count toward her two-hour-a-day limit of total screen time.
- **Set IMing rules.** No IMing, for instance, until homework's finished. Make sure your child knows everyone on his buddy list, and go over the list with him from time to time. Make it clear that sex talk, trash talk, and messages that spread rumors about other kids are never allowed.
- **Keep the computer in a common area.** That way, you can keep an eye on what she's doing, how long she's spending in front of the computer, if she's doing homework or instant messaging, and what other kids are saying.

The key is to minimize the time your child spends chatting online. Help him learn to focus on one thing at a time, not just IMing, and develop the ability to read *people,* not just 160-character online messages.

3. I want to get my kid a cell phone for safety reasons. What kind should I get?

I'm a big believer that most kids should not have a cell phone until they're approaching high school, because they're too much of a distraction and have other downsides that I've discussed earlier. However, if you think it's important for your eleven- or twelve-year-old to have a phone for safety reasons, I'd recommend getting a basic, prepaid mobile phone with no bells and whistles—very limited or no text messaging, no camera, and no Web browsing, downloading, and data plan. The reason is that kids who have advanced smartphones aren't just talking on them, they're going online, playing games, downloading apps and ringtones. They're also taking pictures, recording videos, and texting constantly.

According to Nielsen, a kid age nine to twelve who has a smartphone sends an average of 1,146 texts a month.[3] That's almost forty text messages a day. Like instant messaging, texting is real-time communication, but the difference is that it's mobile and extremely private. Kids text anywhere and everywhere—in school, on the bus, and in bed—usually with no supervision, and it's easy for them to be impulsive and irresponsible. They can send and forward bullying texts or instantly blast embarrassing photos and videos to all their friends. They can also use text messages to cheat in class, silently passing answers from student to student.

And texting too easily becomes a substitute for face-to-face communication. Quick, shorthand text messages—typed on the fly, thumbs zooming over a cell phone keyboard—take less time than conversations and are less complex, with no nuances of body language and facial expression that kids need to process. But when children's eyes are focused on phones instead of human beings, they're not developing and practicing the emotional skills they need to communicate successfully in the real world. So if your eleven- or twelve-year-old needs a cell phone for safety reasons, get her a basic phone instead of a distracting, disruptive, and seductive mobile device.

4. Is it okay for my kid to use Facebook?

At eleven and twelve, kids start feeling a lot of pressure to get on Facebook. Many or most of their classmates may already be on it. Facebook, in fact, is the top online destination of boys who are eight to twelve and girls age twelve to fifteen. Your kid may tell you that he'll feel excluded and uncool if he doesn't have a Facebook page, but I strongly recommend that you say no to Facebook and hold your ground. Your child is still too young—legally, according to Facebook's rules—and much too immature to deal with the intense, often negative and overwhelming pressures of social media.

Let's start with the age issue. Facebook officially bars anyone who's under thirteen from registering for a Facebook account. The site claims that it removes twenty thousand underage users a day.[4] But the fact is, it's ridiculously easy for underage kids to get on Facebook, and too many do. According to *Consumer Reports,* more than 7.5 million members of Facebook were younger than thirteen in 2011.

If your tween wants to get a Facebook account without telling you, all she needs is contact information, an e-mail address, and a fake birth date. Many kids, however, do ask their parents' permission before using Facebook. Parents who agree are letting their kids lie about their age to get on the site. Think about the message that sends to a preteenager. There's really not much difference between using a fake birth date on Facebook and using a fake ID to buy a drink when your kid is underage. Your decision sets a precedent for your child's future behavior.

Facebook's official policy, though, is just one reason why an eleven- or twelve-year-old is too young for Facebook. Studies show that social networking can have serious social and emotional consequences for kids this age. The bottom line is that Facebook can intensify, amplify, and publicize the many insecurities that tweens experience, along with impulsive behavior, cruelty, bullying, and social exclusion. Instead of dealing with these difficult issues in private, with friends and family, preteenagers on Facebook are doing it on a huge, public stage in front of a vast, invisible audience of peers and strangers. They don't have the skills, knowledge, and maturity to be self-protective, and the consequences can be socially and emotionally devastating.

Facebook can also become a habit, setting kids up for problems linked to heavy social networking, from narcissism and depression to isolation and antisocial behavior. And by focusing on online instead of face-to-face communication, kids aren't building their fluency in reading facial expressions, body language, and tone of voice—the emotional skills humans need to succeed in life. Finally, it can be a huge time drain for many kids.

Personally, I think kids shouldn't use Facebook until they're at least fifteen. By that age, they hopefully have enough maturity, perspective, and experience to handle much of the social pressure. Eleven- and twelve-year-old kids, in general, are still too young to understand the rules and risks of growing up in public, as well as the intense and often invasive environment of social media.

5. I just checked my twelve-year-old's browser history and found out he's been looking at online porn. What should I do?
Most tweens are really curious about sex, and these days they can instantly find out and explore just about anything online—intentionally and unintentionally. Even if you've set strict parental controls on your Web browser, X-rated sites can still occasionally slip through, and kids this age often learn about porn sites from other kids. The truth is, you can't shield your kid from all exposure to online pornography; it's just too widespread and easily accessed. But at this age, it's good to have a matter-of-fact conversation with your tween about how easy it is to run into porn on the Internet, how degrading it is to the people involved, and how completely different it is from real-life intimacy. A frank discussion now can keep exposure to porn from distorting your child's understanding and expectations about sexual behavior. Here are some tips:

- Don't shame or interrogate your child. It's a really embarrassing topic, but you don't want your tween to shut down when you talk about porn. Stay straightforward and nonjudgmental so your kid will feel safe talking to you about personal issues.
- Ask your kid what he thinks about any graphic websites he may have seen. Engage him and encourage him to share his

point of view. Talk about any questions that might come up for him.

- Explain that porn is fantasy. Real life, real people, and real relationships aren't like that. It's largely acting and make-believe.

- Talk about how demeaning pornography is to women. Point out that it can turn them into sexual objects and dehumanize them. Explain that women who act that way are in bad places in their lives, and that real intimacy is based on respect and love. Share your values.

- Keep talking. It's not a onetime conversation. Let your child know that you're always there to listen, talk, and answer any questions about sex and intimacy.

- Keep the computer in a common area, and keep checking your child's browser history. If your child knows that *you* know what he's looking at, there's a better chance he'll stay off those sites.

What Parents Need to Know

1. Be a digital role model.

Your kid learns more from what you do than from what you say. So if you want your eleven- or twelve-year-old to use digital media responsibly, set a great example. Turn phones, TV, and other digital technology off during all family meals. Live a balanced life—spend time being active, being outdoors, reading, talking, and doing things with your kid. Get to know her digital world, the music and sites she loves, and what she's experiencing online. And set firm media rules. Make it clear that you're paying attention. Show your child how to use technology safely, productively, and responsibly. And take family "technology time-outs" together so that unplugged time to think, read, play, and imagine is part of your family routine.

2. Teach your kid about digital safety and citizenship.
At Common Sense Media, we stress the importance of teaching kids responsible online behavior—what we call digital citizenship—so they understand the basics of Internet safety and security. This also covers privacy, cyberbullying, copyright, creation, and critical thinking. When kids understand these digital "rules of the road," they can stay safe, protect their privacy, enjoy the positives of digital media, and minimize risks.

As a parent, it's important to talk to your eleven- or twelve-year-old about these safety basics before he starts exploring online more independently:

- **Keep personal information private.** Everything on the Web can be seen by an online audience. Once something is out there, it's out there permanently and can be shared, copied, and changed instantly.
- **Respect other people's privacy.** Never share a friend's private messages or information without asking permission.
- **Use privacy settings.** Make sure they're up-to-date on all devices.
- **Don't share passwords,** ever, and pick ones that other people won't be able to guess.
- **Protect your reputation.** Don't post anything that you wouldn't want your parents, teachers, or friends to see.
- **Treat others online the way you'd want them to treat you.** Never bully, embarrass, or harass someone.
- **Stand up for others.** Never participate in bullying; report bullies and flag cruel online comments.
- **Respect and give credit for other people's work.** Technology makes it easy to copy and paste, but it's wrong to pretend that other people's work is yours.
- **Don't make anonymous comments.** Don't say or do anything online that you would not want to put your name to.
- **Don't cheat.** Cheating is always wrong, even if mobile and digital technology makes it easy.

3. Protect your tween from cyberbullying.

Studies suggest that around 20 percent of tweens have been victims of cyberbullying. It's a serious problem. Eleven- and twelve-year-olds can be cruel to each other, and IMing, texting, and social networking makes it easy for bullies to target and attack kids relentlessly, publicly, and anonymously. The effects can be terrible and tragic. Kids who are cyberbullied are more likely to have low self-esteem, depression, and problems with family and school; they can be afraid to go to class and even have suicidal thoughts.[5] The good news is that there are steps you can take to minimize the chances your child will be a victim or perpetrator of cyberbullying:

- Don't let your eleven- or twelve-year-old use Facebook or other social networks. A recent study found that more than half of all cyberbullying incidents happen on social media.[6]
- Don't give your tween a cell phone with unrestricted text messaging capabilities. Nearly 40 percent of cyberbullying takes place using cell phones and texting.[7]
- Keep the computer and other Internet devices out of your child's bedroom. If your child is being cyberbullied and has online access in her own room, she'll have no escape from the cruel harassment.
- Talk to your child about safe online behavior. Explain that he should never share anything private or do anything that feels uncomfortable. Remind him that it's never appropriate to sext, embarrass anyone, or say hateful things in person or online.
- Teach your kid to stand up for others. If a friend is being cyberbullied, he should never take part. He should flag cruel comments and tell a teacher or other trusted adult.
- Check your kid's online accounts. Read her IMs, social network comments, and texts to see what she and her peers are saying and chatting about. If you don't know

what's going on in your child's life—and tweens are living more and more of their lives online—you won't be able to help.

4. Teach your kid not to believe everything she reads or sees online.

At eleven and twelve, kids are doing online research for school reports and other homework assignments, but it can be hard to wade through the overwhelming amount of information on the Web and find reliable sources. Unfortunately, a lot of kids believe what they see and read online if sites look like they're official. So it's important to teach your tween to have a critical eye and not trust everything he sees, or people he meets, online.

A good place to start is by asking teachers for the school's online research policies and trusted sites they recommend. If your child finds some interesting facts on other sites, make sure he knows that he should always verify the information with other sources. And stress online safety. A recent study found that kids who don't think critically about information are more easily fooled and more likely to trust strangers they encounter online. Be sure your child knows never to respond to any online messages from a screen name she doesn't recognize, even if that person claims to be "a friend of a friend." By learning to be cautious online, your kid can steer clear of false information, rumors, and predators hiding behind false identities.

5. Encourage your child's digital creativity.

Digital devices can be efficient tools and entertainment platforms, as well as time wasters, but they can also inspire tweens' imagination and creativity.

With a simple digital camera, your kid can explore the fun of photography. And with free photo editing software and apps, he can experiment with endless cool, crazy effects. Sites like Cartoon Network Game Center and Disney Go let kids build and play online games and make their own comics. With mobile apps like Toontastic, Storykit, and Reel Director, kids can create their own animations, and Beatwave and VoiceBot help them compose original music. When kids use digital media to express themselves imaginatively, instead of consuming prepackaged entertainment, they build skills and confidence, as well as new ways of seeing themselves and the world around them.

Ages Thirteen to Fifteen

Young and mid-teens are in the throes of change—physical, emotional, and social. As their bodies are maturing rapidly, hormonal surges are triggering mood swings, emotional drama, and sexual experimentation. These transformations are tough enough to deal with in the privacy of family or in face-to-face interactions with friends and classmates. But when they're manifested online, in front of large, faceless, sometimes hostile audiences, their intensity and impact can be hugely amplified.

As parents, it's vital to set clear boundaries and expectations for thirteen- to fifteen-year-olds and give them the tools to stay safe online and offline. Now that they're teens, they have fewer restrictions on where they go and what they can do, but young teens, especially, still lack the maturity to make all the right choices in new, challenging situations. They're trying on different personas and living in a vast digital world. Many are using social media or watching videos of their peers on YouTube—engaging in everything from girl fights to reenactments of *Jackass* stunts—that can normalize risky, antisocial behavior. The result can be lots of intensity with friends and love interests that may get magnified and distorted when it goes online.

But teens are also having lots of positive digital media experiences.

They're engaging with their communities and the world, and technology can open a lot of doors for their talents and passions. Their opportunities to discover and connect are almost limitless, and there can be great educational benefits. As parents, we need to help them minimize the risks and reap the benefits. The answers and tips below can help you guide them.

What Parents Want to Know

1. Should I let my kid have a Facebook account?

Once your kid turns thirteen, it's officially okay for her to have an account on Facebook, but that doesn't mean it has to be okay with you. My personal opinion is that kids shouldn't have Facebook pages until they're at least fifteen, when they have a bit more social and life experience to buffer the pressures and avoid the problems that young kids often get into on social media. But the fact is, your teen—whether thirteen, fourteen, or fifteen—is likely to feel uncool and left out if he's not Facebooking like most of his friends, and he may set up an account without telling you.

Don't get me wrong: many teens have a positive experience with social media. They use it to stay connected with friends and family, build a sense of community, and express their feelings, thoughts, and identity. A lot of schools are letting students use Facebook to collaborate on homework. But every positive use can also have a negative flipside. And because Facebook amplifies and broadcasts everything you post, bad experiences can be very, very bad. The younger kids are, the less judgment they have and the less prepared and aware they are about the risks and perils of social networks. That's why I strongly advise waiting until your child is at least a mid-teen before letting him get a Facebook page.

Here are some of the specific Facebook-related issues to keep in mind:

- **The pressure to measure up.** Being able to see how many "friends" your peers have, and who they are, makes it all too easy to compare yourself and worry about being excluded. That's especially true when kids post about their social activities. If your kid finds out on Facebook that she wasn't invited to a party, it's going to be especially painful because everybody else on Facebook will know it, too. The American Academy of Pediatrics recently warned that kids with low self-esteem run the risk of "Facebook depression" when they see their peers' profiles filled with happy photos and updates, and they assume that they're the only ones who are feeling sad. Social networks magnify and intensify normal teenage emotions, including social anxiety, jealousy, insecurity, and fear of rejection. Make sure your child is strong and mature enough to handle these issues on a public, online stage before using Facebook.

- **The problem of oversharing.** Teens, especially young teens, can be impulsive. They often don't have a strong sense of privacy boundaries—except, of course, when it comes to parents—and little grasp of the consequences of posting information that could be used against them and damage their reputation. Without thinking or stopping to edit themselves, they can post comments that can hurt people or pictures of themselves—holding a beer bottle or posing provocatively, for example. These images may stay on the Internet forever and be shared and seen by huge numbers of people, including school officials or college admissions officers. In short, they can come back to bite them embarrassingly in the future. Before your teen gets a Facebook account, make sure he knows that he should never post anything that he wouldn't say to someone's face or would not want his parents, teachers, or future employers to see.

- **The risk of becoming a target.** Bullying has always been a problem, but when it's online, in public—using technology that can broadcast anonymous slurs with incredible speed and momentum—its effect can be much more destructive. When someone posts a comment like "Why are you so fat?" or "People just pretend to like you" on your teen's Facebook page, where everyone can see it, it's especially cruel and can even generate mob behavior. Other people can at times post hateful taunts just to join in. Like everything else, cruelty and vicious gossip spread rapidly and powerfully on social networks. This is particularly true with apps like Honesty Box and The Bathroom Wall, sites like Formspring.me, About Everyone.com and Topix that let users post anonymous comments. Make sure your teen is sturdy enough to handle the risk of cyberbullying, knows not to participate, and knows what to do if it happens before she uses social media.

If you decide that your child is mature enough to have a Facebook page, it's a good idea to discuss and agree, beforehand, on ground rules to keep her online social life safe and under control:

- **Friend your child.** That way you'll know what she and her friends are posting, and it may help her think twice before she shares something, because you'll be able to see it. Of course, your teen may figure out how to block you or set up a second Facebook account that you don't know about, so don't assume you know everything that's going on. Make sure you check in with her face-to-face about how things are going and don't rely on her status updates for information.
- **Use the strictest privacy settings.** Sit down with your teen and go over Facebook's privacy options. Make sure that any posts and information are shared with his "Friends" only. Also remind your teen that he should approve any photos or posts that he's tagged in before they link to his page, and that he's notified when there's any activity in his name.
- **Set rules about posting.** Explain that it's never okay for your teen to post sexy photos, pictures of himself drinking, or anything that could hurt someone else or his own reputation.
- **Set time limits.** Whether your teen is Facebooking for fun or homework, it still counts toward her daily limit on screen time.
- **Keep the computer in a common area.** That way, you can keep an eye on your teen's Facebooking as well as the clock.

2. Should I let my kid have a smartphone?

Teens are under huge pressure to have smartphones with unlimited texting and data plans. Most of their friends probably do, and texting is the only way many of them seem to communicate. Actually *talking* on the phone is so old school. Thirteen- to seventeen-year-olds text more than any other age group. And kids text everywhere—at school, in the mall, on the bus, at home, and in bed when they're supposed to be sleeping. According to a 2010 study, nearly half of all teens who take their phones to school send a text while they're in class at least once a day.[1]

Texting can be both impulsive and compulsive. It's easy for kids to lose control of the messages they're frantically typing and the amount of time and attention they're giving to their phones instead of more important things in life—like homework, safety, and face-to-face communication.

Teens love texting because they can be instantly in touch with friends, no matter where they are. But the rapid-fire exchanges can mean that kids don't take the time to think before they push the "send" button. Without the help of facial expressions, body language, and tone of voice, words on a screen can seem harsh, insulting, or ill-considered. They can also be saved and shared publicly, without permission. Once you send a text message or photo, you lose control of it. And some teens use texting to hurt or humiliate other people. It's easy to snap an embarrassing photo with a smartphone and text it to dozens of people, and taunting, hateful messages can do psychic damage. Smartphones are powerful communication platforms, and in immature hands, they can create havoc.

Too much texting is a problem, too. When kids have their eyes glued on their cell phones, they're not paying attention to people and what's going on around them. When they're texting and doing homework, they're not retaining everything that they're supposed to be learning, and they're often spending much longer on assignments than they should be.

And phones in school can be a temptation to cheat. Nearly 70 percent of schools prohibit cell phone use, but most kids ignore those rules. More than 35 percent of them say they've used their cell phones to cheat—by texting quiz answers to their friends, photographing and sending them pictures of exam questions, and going online to find answers when they're taking a test.

With a smartphone and data plan, kids also have instant access to lots of apps that encourage risky choices and behavior. The Android Market, for example, features tons of cheap drug-related apps like Garden of Weeden, which teaches users how to grow pot, and Nose Candy, which provides step-by-step, illustrated instructions for using cocaine. The iTunes App Store offers apps like Meet New People, which enable and encourage users to flirt with strangers. The bottom line is that a smartphone is much more than a phone. It's a pocket-sized, portable Internet device that kids can use privately, with little or no supervision.

So, especially if you have a younger teen, think carefully about the distraction and risks of handing him a smartphone. The older the child, the better. I personally think kids should be in high school before they have one, and that's the rule in our family.

If you decide that your teen is ready to use one, though, set clear ground rules first, as well as consequences for breaking them, and reinforce them often. Here's what I recommend:

- **Understand everything the phone can do before you give it to your child.** Trust me, your teen will figure it all out, so you should know its capabilities and restrict, disable, or refuse to pay for any features you don't want her to use, like texting and going online. Just because her friends do it doesn't mean she has to.
- **Be clear about what, and when, it's okay to text.** Make sure your kid understands how to use the phone responsibly. If you've decided that unlimited texting is okay, your teen should know to stop and think before he hits the "send" button, and that he should never send sexual or harassing texts. He should also know and always obey school rules about phone use, and that he should *never* cheat. Set overall family rules, too, about cell phone use—no phones at any meals,

for example, or in the bedroom—and set firm consequences, like losing phone privileges, for breaking them.

- **Tell your teen that you reserve the right to check the messages and photos on her phone if she doesn't seem to be following the rules.** It might feel like snooping, but her cell phone is a privilege that you're paying for, and it's your job as a parent to make sure she's safe.

3. I found a sexually suggestive photo on my daughter's phone. What should I do about it?

Have a talk right away with your kid about the real hazards and consequences of sexting—sending sexually explicit photos or messages by texting. If the photo on her phone is provocative but not revealing, there's a good chance that talking to her will keep her from doing something that could be very harmful to her life.

Unfortunately, sexting is increasingly common. A fifth of teen girls and boys have sent photos of themselves naked or semi-nude over their phones or the Internet. Girls, especially, can feel a lot of social pressure to sext. Boys will ask them to send a revealing picture, and girls will do it to get or keep their attention. Many think the photo will stay private, but nothing's truly private once it goes online. A boy will show it to his friends, and they'll pass it on. Even if a girl sexts her boyfriend as a token of love, the image can easily become public if they break up. One girl had an explicit video she sent to her boyfriend posted on the school's computer—everybody saw it, including the principal. The results can be overwhelming and can even cause a teen to try to take her life.

Sexting can also lead to criminal prosecution. It's illegal to send sexual images to minors, and kids in some states have been charged with child pornography and felony obscenity for texting. It's clearly nothing to play around with, even if some teens think it's harmless, a form of "safe sex," or a way to look cool. Your daughter might not think about, or know, the consequences. The most important thing you can do is make sure that she does.

4. My kid has a fit when we want him to stop gaming and get off the Internet, and he barely holds a conversation with us anymore. What should we do?

For some teens—perhaps one in twenty-five, according to a recent study[2]—Internet use can be "problematic." It's hard for them to pull themselves away from games, with their attention-grabbing action and graphics, and the consuming virtual worlds of chat rooms and social networks. A study by Dr. Dimitri Christakis at the University of Washington found that "problematic Internet use" is more common than asthma among college students, and teenagers are more prone to it than any other age group.[3]

It's not something to ignore, even if your kid snarls or yells at you when you tell him to get off the computer. Problematic Internet use is a form of dependency—kids who exhibit it feel tense, anxious, and distressed when they're not online. Christakis also found that they're prone to depression; another recent study suggests they're more likely to behave aggressively, smoke, and use drugs than other kids.[4] No research has found a direct link, but experts believe that kids who are unsure of themselves socially are more prone to become dependent on the engrossing alternative reality that the Internet offers. It can be less stressful and socially challenging than real life, but it's also extremely isolating. The more time they spend living virtually online, the less they're developing the interpersonal skills, coping mechanisms, and confidence they need in the real world. The Internet becomes their most important relationship. It's basically a vicious cycle.

So pay close attention. If your teen gets irritable, angry, or depressed when he's not online, he may have a dependency. Have a serious talk with him about your concerns and encourage him to get outside, involved in other activities, and engaged in life. Try to gradually limit his time in front of the computer, but don't take it away, because withdrawal can cause harmful reactions, including depression. It may be a good idea to talk to a professional; ask your child's doctor or school counselor for advice. Problematic Internet use may signal underlying problems that require professional help.

5. My son loves to play ultra-violent M-rated games where he uses the controller as a knife to decapitate people. Is there anything I can do to discourage this?

Exploding body parts; death by cleaver, shotgun, sword, and chain saw; ripping out opponents' hearts and spines with your bare hands— M-rated games are awash in blood and brutal, graphic violence. These killing games, in which the players role play murder and massacre, can also include repulsive, extreme sexual violence. In Mortal Kombat, for example, the player can assume the role of a sexual torturer, raping a female, urinating on her, soaking her with gasoline and setting her on fire, then ripping her body in half from her genitals to her head.

This is not kid stuff. In fact, M-rated games, like X-rated, NC-17 movies, are rated for those seventeen and up. Your child may be more independent at thirteen, fourteen, or fifteen, but you're still the parent, and you set the rules. You wouldn't let your son watch X-rated movies at home, and you shouldn't allow him to play ultra-violent M-rated video games either.

Many retailers won't sell these games to kids under seventeen without their parents' permission, but younger kids can still play them if their parents, friends, and older siblings and cousins allow it. But that's a bad decision. Studies show that when kids are exposed to media violence— especially bloody, brutal, first-person killer games—they're more likely to act aggressively, become insensitive to violence and its victims, and see it as a normal way of resolving conflict. As the American Academy of Pediatrics puts it, "Playing violent video games leads to adolescent violence like smoking leads to lung cancer."

The simplest approach is a zero-tolerance policy for M-rated games at this age. Like X-rated movies, they should be completely out of bounds for underage kids. Have a talk with your son about the consequences of real violence. Ask him how he'd feel if someone he cared about was a victim, and explain what happens in real life to people who commit violence. Set your house rules: no M-rated gaming allowed, period. Explain why and then enforce consequences. Keep the computer and gaming device in a common area, where you can see what your kid's playing, and watch out for online games, which aren't covered by the rating system and can be very violent.

What Parents Need to Know

1. Privacy is a huge deal. Teach your kid to think before hitting the "send" button—to self-reflect before she self-reveals.
Your teen needs to understand that there are no secrets online. Messages and photos exchanged "just between friends" can suddenly, easily be blasted across the Internet, reaching dozens, hundreds, or thousands of other people. Once you hit the "send" button on your cell phone or computer, you lose control, so it's essential to teach her to take control of her words and images while she can, before she posts.

Remind your kid that she's creating a permanent record and image on the Internet that will stick to her and that other people can see—college admissions officers, for example. Seventy percent of colleges check applicants' Facebook pages as part of the admission process,[5] and a Google search can turn up stuff about her that she didn't even know was out there. These days, your teen's online postings and pictures may be the first impression he makes on schools and employers. Here are key tips to make sure that it's a good one:

- Your teen should ensure that his social network profile isn't publicly searchable. He should go to the Facebook privacy settings, for example, and check that his page is visible to "Friends" only.
- Teach your kid to take a deep breath and reflect before she posts, texts, or tweets. She should ask herself why she's posting the message or photo, who might be able to see it, whether they could misunderstand it, and whether someone could use it against her. Once it's out there, she can't take it back.
- To really get the message across, try this test with your teen: go online and search for information about each other on the

Internet. Check any links and write down all the information that's out there about each other. You and your kid might both be surprised—or shocked—by the things people can learn about you online, both true and false.

2. Make sure your teen understands appropriate online behavior and that cyberbullying and other forms of digital harassment are never okay.

Kids between thirteen and fifteen are more likely to encounter cyberbullying than other age groups. So it's really important that your teen knows what's okay and what's not okay to do and say when he's online. Smartphones, social networks, and anonymous posts give kids who are acting out the tools to be cruel and publicly torment others in ways that can be devastating in their scale and impact. Digital harassment can be difficult for victims to escape, and it can destroy their lives.

Here's what your thirteen- to fifteen-year-old needs to understand:

- Never participate in cyberbullying. If you know someone's doing it, tell a trusted adult and help the victim.
- Never do anything, online or offline, that makes you feel creepy or uncomfortable. That includes sending sexy photos, sharing passwords, or spending too much time scrutinizing someone else's Facebook page.
- Understand that the privilege of having powerful digital devices comes with responsibilities. Never abuse the privilege by using them inappropriately or to abuse others.

3. Talk to your kid about not using location-sharing services like Facebook Places.

Teens are living a lot of their lives online, but new location-sharing programs—like Foursquare, Loopt, Gowalla, and Facebook Places—cross a boundary, in my opinion. They let users post their physical location and broadcast where they are to friends, marketers, and, in some cases, users they don't know.

There are a couple of reasons why your teen shouldn't sign up for these services. The first is safety. If the strictest privacy settings aren't selected—allowing only close friends to see location postings—there's a risk that someone could potentially use the information to stalk your child. Another problem is advertising. Marketers use these services to send targeted ads to users when they "check in" to places, offering deals and other persuasive encouragements to spend.

So be careful. I personally wouldn't feel comfortable letting my fourteen- or fifteen-year-old use location sharing—it's one more way technology is crossing new privacy boundaries, and I worry about the risk to my kids' personal safety. If you don't know if your teen is using geolocation services, you can check her phone to see if she's downloaded the apps. If she has, talk to her to make sure she's got the strictest privacy settings and caution her not to post her location when she's alone.

4. Take technology time-outs.

Even though your kid's a teen and getting more independent, it's important to unplug and enforce time limits on digital media. When your child spends more than two hours a day in front of a screen, he's spending less time than he should in the real world, being active, and developing his inner resources. And according to a recent study, kids up to age eighteen who spend more time with media have lower grades and less personal contentment than other kids. Heavy users are more likely to get Cs or lower in school, to be bored and sad, and to get into trouble.[6]

So don't loosen up—time limits still matter, a lot. Stick to your rules, unplug as a family, and help your kid plan how to use her daily digital media diet productively.

5. Help your kid create a responsible digital life that takes advantage of the new educational opportunities and complements his life in the real world.

There's no question that digital media provides extraordinary new opportunities for creativity, collaboration, and connectedness, and it's important that every kid has a chance to take advantage of these remarkable resources. From new forms of online research to learning and sharing music skills on YouTube, it's great to encourage your teen and her teachers to access the remarkable potential of technology for learning and creativity.

It's also vital to encourage your kid to be a safe, smart, responsible digital citizen, striking a healthy balance between time spent online and in the real world and always behaving ethically and responsibly toward others. Digital media offers almost limitless challenges and opportunities for learning and self-expression. Teaching your child how to use them wisely can make all the difference in the world.

Talking Back and Taking Back Control

When I first decided to write this book, my own kids were predictably aghast. They didn't really like the attention the book might draw to them. They didn't want me to share personal stories, which they feel are overly stereotypical of themselves and their friends. And they just wished I had better things to do with my time. Words like "Oh no" and "embarrassing" cropped up many times.

That said, our three older kids openly acknowledged that these were serious issues in their lives and those of their friends and classmates. Indeed, my concerns about video game addiction, the social and emotional consequences of unhealthy uses of Facebook, and the extraordinary learning potential of digital platforms are all deeply rooted in my personal experience as a parent and educator.

During the months in which I researched and wrote this book, a funny thing happened. My kids started saying, in their own unique ways, that maybe it wasn't such a bad idea that Dad was writing this book. That my concerns were actually very real. That both the perils and possibilities of this rapidly evolving digital age needed to be explained in pretty simple terms for the average family. That young people and their parents needed to get a better handle on how Facebook, cell phones, iPads, and the like were affecting our lives.

In short, even my own long-suffering kids started to reinforce my belief that millions of parents, educators, and young people out there need some guidance and that all of us need to feel empowered to deal with the phenomenal changes that have happened at warp speed. Because at the end of the day, that's what really matters. Facebook, smartphones, YouTube, and who knows what other forms of digital media are here to stay. The key is that we—as parents, educators, and citizens—take back control for the sake of our own families and the broader society.

I know that many parents feel helpless and voiceless in dealing with Facebook and the 24/7 digital world it represents. These new platforms present major challenges and important opportunities for raising children and teens. But many parents and teachers feel somewhat alone and powerless in their concerns and their frustrations about how Facebook, Twitter, YouTube, et al. are affecting their children's ways of relating to themselves and others. The speed of change has simply been so rapid that many parents, including myself at times, feel blindsided by their impact. We're not prepared to handle them like other parenting responsibilities, because we didn't grow up with these platforms. And frankly, most of us hadn't seen these extraordinary changes coming. Suddenly, they were upon us, like a runaway train. We had to deal with them as best we could, as did many leaders and institutions who traditionally might have helped regulate or mediate their impact.

But parents have the right, indeed, the obligation, to speak up and be heard. They also have the right and, I would argue, the responsibility to assert control over how they raise their children and help their kids make proper choices, even about new, unfamiliar technology platforms. The good news is that the tide slowly seems to be turning. As a country, we are starting to apply some brakes to this runaway train, and we are starting to get a handle on the impacts on our kids, both pro and con, and how best to deal with them. We are learning that we *can* take back control, and we are starting to do so.

As I mentioned in the introduction, I included Facebook in the title of this book for a reason. To me, it represents perhaps the most potent symbol of this digital revolution and the impact it's having on kids and teens. Like it or not, Facebook is the eight-hundred-pound gorilla of the digital media revolution where young people are concerned, and the company and its leadership should have a unique sense of responsibility and accountability to all of us, especially kids.

Just before I turned in the final manuscript for this book, Facebook agreed to a groundbreaking twenty-year privacy settlement with the U.S. government. This public policy milestone hopefully began to shift the privacy debate in favor of consumers and kids. According to its settlement with the Federal Trade Commission, Facebook is now required to obtain its users' permission *before* changing their privacy controls and how their personal information is released and shared. This shift to an opt-in standard is very significant. In addition, Facebook is now required to submit to regular privacy audits by independent third parties for the next twenty years.

This settlement, which the *Wall Street Journal* referred to as "the strongest government rebuke yet to the social network,"[1] is by no means the full answer to many of the concerns we should all have about Facebook and other digital media platforms. Its requirement that Facebook's users be permitted to "opt-in" to new privacy changes is only prospective. It doesn't account for the myriad and repeated privacy violations that have happened to date. And it does not require Facebook to restore the privacy settings it rolled back in 2009, which led to the FTC's complaint in the first place. Nor can this or any regulation deal with the unfortunate ways in which Facebook and other digital platforms encourage young people to self-reveal, often in painful and embarrassing ways, before they self-reflect. In short, we need to develop much stronger regulation and much broader public education efforts on these topics as soon as possible.

Yet this settlement is very important and highly symbolic nonetheless. It is the first major governmental action that clearly states that we as consumers do have the power and control over our private information. Moreover, Mark Zuckerberg's accompanying mea culpa to the settlement agreement—in a blog post, of course—demonstrates that he and his colleagues may finally be acknowledging some accountability on the privacy front. All of this is critical, because we as parents and citizens should not feel powerless or helpless or at the mercy of uncontrollable technology platforms.

Hopefully, this book will help give parents, and all citizens, some of the knowledge and tools we need to take back control from Facebook, the other social networks, and the data-driven engineers who have helped spawn this extraordinary digital revolution we are living through. The voices and wisdom of parents should be a critical part of this conversation. And our voices need to be central to the growing national debate about what's appropriate and healthy for our children and families.

It's time that we all started talking back to Facebook . . . and taking back control of the most important job we do: raising our kids.

Acknowledgments

This book, like virtually everything I work on, has been a collaborative process. While I am entirely responsible for the final product, I couldn't have done it without the great support and input of many friends, colleagues, and family.

First and foremost, I've had a wonderful partner in Susan Wels, who collaborated with me from the beginning, just as she did on my first book, *The Other Parent*. Susan has been a great friend since college, and she is a terrific author and superb editor. Her wisdom and good judgment are evident in every aspect of the book, and I couldn't have chosen a better colleague. The book is truly a team effort, and I can't thank Susan enough for her invaluable partnership.

Chelsea Clinton has also been an exceptionally talented and valued colleague from the outset. In addition to her thoughtful foreword, Chelsea also contributed many insights and much support. Chelsea is an incredibly bright and talented young woman with a grace and maturity that is an extraordinary testament to her entire family. Watching her grow into the remarkable person that she has become has been a joy for her former professor. Chelsea is wise and thoughtful beyond her years, and her contributions to this book were invaluable. She will do many great things in the years ahead.

Not surprisingly, I relied on a number of my colleagues at Common Sense Media in crafting a readable book about such a complex topic. Nobody was more important than my dear friend and longtime partner, Liz Perle, who is a cofounder of Common Sense. As all who know her well can attest, Liz is a remarkably talented and gifted woman, whose courage in the face of life's challenges knows no bounds. A terrific author in her own right, Liz offered many valuable insights, constructive comments, and great support.

Shira Lee Katz and Kelly Schryver of Common Sense Media's education team also made significant contributions to the book. Shira, who has her doctorate in education from Harvard, added thoughtful input, and her understanding of the latest research was invaluable. Kelly, who wrote her senior honors thesis on Facebook and body image, provided a recent graduate's insights into young people's use of social networks and helped immeasurably with fact-checking and editing. Both deserve great thanks. I also benefited from some very good work by several of my Stanford students. Three in particular, Robbie Zimbroff, Brianna Pang, and Nabila Abdullah, helped their professor with everything from interviews of young people to summarizing the latest research in the field.

Two editorial leaders at Common Sense, Jill Murphy and Caroline Knorr, contributed significant insights, especially to the recommendations for parents. In addition, a number of my key colleagues at Common Sense deserve a shout-out for their insights and support. These include cofounder Linda Burch, Amy Shenkan, Colby Zintl, and board leaders Bill Price and Lawrence Wilkinson. Perhaps most of all, I received great help from my trusted and loyal executive assistant, Carina Mifuel, who skillfully helped shepherd every aspect of the book with her usual good cheer and unwavering thoughtfulness.

The book also benefited enormously from the wisdom and input of some longtime friends and colleagues. None was more important than my good friend Ken Auletta, the brilliant best-selling author and *New Yorker* columnist, who provided invaluable insights into the tech industry and into the motivations and psyches of its leaders. In addition, Howard Gardner, whose extraordinary vision and remarkable contributions to the fields of education and child development are world renowned, made enormous contributions to my thinking and to our broader education work at Common Sense. I am proud to call Howard a friend and colleague.

Several widely respected scholars and writers provided invaluable insights through interviews and meetings. Sherry Turkle, the esteemed researcher and author from MIT, was particularly helpful, and her superb book, *Alone Together,* significantly influenced my thinking on broader topics.

I also gained important insights and perspectives from two Stanford colleagues and friends, communications professor Cliff Nass and medical school professor Dr. Elias Aboujaoude, who were very generous with their time and insights. Similarly, the book benefited greatly from lengthy interviews with Dr. Dimitri Christakis of the University of Washington and from the input of Pulitzer Prize–winning *New York Times* reporter Matt Richtel. In addition, best-selling authors David Sheff and Eli Pariser offered significant insights and commentary that helped to shape the book.

On the policy and political front, I want to single out two extraordinary colleagues and friends from Washington, D.C.: Julius Genachowski, the chairman of the FCC, and Jon Leibowitz, the chairman of the FTC. Both have demonstrated critically important leadership for kids and families during the past few years. They have headed up the two most important government agencies regarding media and technology during the Obama administration, and needless to say, parents across this nation owe them a debt of gratitude for their leadership. In addition, Alec Ross, senior adviser for innovation to Secretary of State Hillary Clinton, also offered his usual valuable insights.

A number of good friends encouraged me through the process of writing the book in 2011, including Gary Knell, Matt James, Bill Morrison, Vicky Rideout, Geoff Cowan, Bob Miller, Craig Hatkoff, and Jane Rosenthal. In addition, Vanessa and Aaron Cornell, Susan and Doug

Burrows, Jodi and Tim Carter, Georgia Montgomery, Christy Tripp, Susan Alexander, and Jordana Freeman kindly shared their parenting experiences with us. And I also want to thank the great supporters of Common Sense Media, especially Pierre and Pam Omidyar and the team at the Omidyar Network, whose long-term and incredibly generous investment in our work for kids helped make Common Sense's success and this entire book possible.

My agent, Kris Dahl of ICM, has been a terrific ally for more than a decade and was a wonderful adviser throughout. She brought me to my editors at Scribner, the remarkable Nan Graham and her talented colleague, Paul Whitlatch, and their insights and editing skills have been superb. I owe each of them a great debt of thanks.

Finally, I want to thank and acknowledge my family, starting with my two brothers, Hume and Tom. Their longstanding love and support is a hugely important part of my life. As you would imagine, my four children, Lily, Kirk, Carly, and Jesse, contributed greatly to the book. They were not only my true inspiration for writing it in the first place, but each of my kids critiqued it in their own special ways, and each added unique insights, commentary, and firsthand lessons in parenting. I love them all more than anything . . . and I hope they're proud of the book.

And finally, my extraordinary wife, Liz, has been my life partner and best friend for more than twenty years. I love and thank her ever so much.

Notes

Introduction

1 The Nielsen Company, "U.S. Teen Mobile Report: Calling Yesterday, Texting Today, Using Apps Tomorrow," Nielsen Wire, October 14, 2010; accessed at http://blog.nielsen.com/nielsenwire/online_mobile/u-s-teen-mobile-report -calling-yesterday-texting-today-using-apps-tomorrow/ on November 6, 2011.

2 Kaiser Family Foundation Study, "Generation M," January 2010.

3 See www.CommonSense.org/Educators.

Chapter One: Relationships: Connection, Intimacy, and Self-Image

1 Jonathan Franzen, "Liking Is for Cowards. Go for What Hurts," *New York Times*, May 29, 2011, op ed.

2 Interview with Cliff Nass, May 19, 2011, at Stanford University.

3 Sherry Turkle, *Alone Together* (New York: Basic Books, 2011).

4 Ibid., p. 268.

5 Interview with Cliff Nass, June 19, 2011, at Stanford University, and Joan Hamilton, "Separation Anxiety," *Stanford Magazine*, January/February 2011, p. 3.

6 See also stories and commentary in Turkle, *Alone Together*, pp. 266–68.

Notes

7 Interview with Sherry Turkle, July 11, 2011, and see her book *Alone Together.*

8 Turkle, *Alone Together,* pp. 180–83, stories from various teens.

9 Ibid., pp. 179–80.

10 Jaron Lanier, *You Are Not a Gadget: A Manifesto* (New York: Vintage, 2010).

11 "State of the Net 2010," *Consumer Reports Magazine,* June 2010.

12 Jonathan Franzen, "Liking Is for Cowards. Go for What Hurts," *New York Times,* May 29, 2011, op ed.

13 Interview with Dr. Elias Aboujaoude, *Stanford Magazine,* January/February 2011; phone interview with Dr. Aboujaoude, June 9, 2011. See also Joan Hamilton, "Separation Anxiety."

14 Cliff Nass's research was discussed during a personal interview on May 19, 2011, at Stanford University. The research will be formally released in 2012.

15 Kelly Schryver, "Keeping Up Appearances," 2011 honors thesis, Brown University.

16 See Eg. Csipke & Horne, 2007, Day & Keys, 2008 and Harper, Sperry & Thompson, 2008. All cited in Kelly Schryver's honors thesis.

17 Schryver, "Keeping Up Appearances."

18 "Cyberbullying and Online Teens," AP-MTV Digital Abuse Study, 2009.

19 D. A. Gentile, H. Choo, A. Liau, T. Sim, D. Li, D. Fung, and A. Khoo, "Pathological Video Game Use Among Youths: A Two-Year Longitudinal Study," *Pediatrics* 127, no. 2 (2011): E319–29.

20 L. T. Lam and Z.-W. Peng, "Effect of Pathological Use of the Internet on Adolescent Mental Health: A Prospective Study," *Archives of Pediatrics and Adolescent Medicine* 164, no. 10 (2010): 901–906.

21 Study by the Peer Research Center and the Annenberg School of Communications at the University of Pennsylvania conducted in October/November 2010 as reported in Benny Evangelista, "Facebook Can Bring Friends, Trust, Support," *San Francisco Chronicle,* June 18, 2011.

22 Interview with Howard Gardner, July 11, 2011.

Chapter Two: Attention and Addiction Issues: Your Child's Brain on Computers

1 Dimitri A. Christakis, MD, MPH; Frederick J. Zimmerman, PhD; David L. DeGiuseppe; and Carolyn A. MacCarty, PhD, "Early Television Exposure

190

and Subsequent Attentional Problems in Children," *Pediatrics* 113, no. 4. (2004): 708–715.

2 Nicholas Carr, *The Shallows: What the Internet Is Doing to Our Brains* (New York: Norton, 2010).

3 Ibid., p. 10.

4 Ibid., pp. 24–35.

5 Interview with Matt Richtel, May 13, 2011.

6 Paul Atchley opinion reported in Matt Richtel, "Outdoors and Out of Reach, Studying the Brain," *New York Times,* August 15, 2010.

7 Interview with Dimitri Christakis, August 3, 2011.

8 Interview with Cliff Nass, June 19, 2011, and as reported in Joan Hamilton, "Separation Anxiety," *Stanford Magazine,* January/February 2011.

9 This summary is drawn from Carr, *The Shallows,* pp. 123–43, as well as conversations with Matt Richtel and Cliff Nass.

10 Matt Richtel, "Driven to Distraction," *New York Times,* series 2009.

11 Stephanie Brown, as quoted in Hamilton, "Separation Anxiety."

12 Byron Reeves, as quoted in Hamilton, "Separation Anxiety."

13 Interview with David Sheff, July 13, 2011, San Francisco, California.

14 Sherry Turkle, *Alone Together* (New York: Basic Books, 2011), pp. 194–206, and interview on July 11, 2011.

15 Interview with Dimitri Christakis, August 3, 2011.

16 Interview with Sherry Turkle, July 11, 2011.

17 Interview with David Sheff, July 13, 2011, San Francisco, California.

Chapter Three: The Loss of Privacy: Why Your Child Is at Risk

1 Mark Zuckerberg as quoted in an interview with *Tech Crunch* in 2010. See "Zuckerberg's Privacy Stance: Facebook CEO Doesn't Believe in Privacy," Huffington Post, Tech, April 29, 2010.

2 Jan Hoffman, "A Girl's Nude Photo, and Altered Lives," *New York Times,* March 27, 2011.

3 Eric Schmidt, video interview with Maria Bartiromo, CNBC, December 3, 2009.

4 Eric Schmidt, quoted in Holman Jenkins, "Google and the Search of Future," *Wall Street Journal,* September 3, 2010.

5 Common Sense Media commissioned two national, scientific polls. The first poll, concerning posting online information, was conducted by Joel Benenson and the Benenson Strategy Group in August 2009. The second poll, about friends' behavior, was conducted by Zogby International in August 2010.

6 Jaron Lanier, as paraphrased in Jennifer Kahn, "The Visionary," *New Yorker*, July 11 and 18, 2011.

7 MTV and the Associated Press, "2011 AP-MTV Digital Abuse Study," 2011.

8 Jan Hoffman, "A Girl's Nude Photo, and Altered Lives," *New York Times*, March 26, 2011.

9 Jenna Wortham, "Your Life on Facebook in Total Recall," *New York Times*, December 15, 2011.

10 Michaelle Bond, "Facebook Timeline a New Privacy Test," *USA Today*, December 11, 2011.

11 Benny Evangelista, "Facebook Changes Will Share Even More Data," *San Francisco Chronicle*, October 2, 2011.

12 Both the Facebook facial recognition story and the Google example are reported in Kevin O'Brien, "Germany Investigating Facebook Tagging Feature," *New York Times*, August 3, 2011.

13 Nick Bilton, "Hackers Claim to Have PlayStation Users' Card Data," *New York Times*, April 28, 2011, Bits blog.

14 For a good article on this, see Cecilia Kang, "Parting with Privacy with a Quick Click," *Washington Post*.

15 Steve Stecklow, "On the Web, Children Face Intensive Tracking," *Wall Street Journal*, September 17, 2010.

16 Danah Boyd, Eszter Hargittai, Jason Schultz, and John Palfrey, "Why Parents Help Their Children Lie to Facebook about Age: Unintended Consequences of the Children's Online Privacy Act," *First Monday*, November 7, 2011.

17 Julie Brill, Federal Trade Comission, *Privacy: A Lesson from the Playroom*, December 6, 2011, http://ftc.gov/speeches/brill/111206iappdraft.pdf.

18 See "Facebook 'Unfair' on Privacy," *Wall Street Journal*, November 20, 2011, p. B1, for a complete summary of the settlement.

19 "President Obama Doesn't Let His Daughter Use Facebook," *Los Angeles Times*, December 15, 2011.

Chapter Four: The End of Innocence

1 For a fuller account, see "Kiki Kannibal: The Girl Who Played with Fire," *Rolling Stone,* April 28, 2011.

2 David Brooks, "The Saga of Sister Kiki," *New York Times,* June 23, 2011, op ed.

3 For an excellent discussion of "age compression" and sexuality, see Diane Levin and Jean Kilbourne, *So Sexy So Soon* (New York: Ballantine Books, 2008), pp. 69–70.

4 "Porn" is the fifth most searched-for term for kids ages six to seventeen. Research study conducted in 2009 by Norton Online Family.

5 J. D. Brown and K. L. L'Engle, "X-Rated: Sexual Attitudes and Behaviors Associated with U.S. Early Adolescents' Exposure to Sexually Explicit Media," *Communication Research* 36, no. 1 (2009): 129–51.

6 See, for example, Kaiser Family Foundation study, *Sex on TV* (Menlo Park, Calif.: Kaiser Family Foundation), p. 1.

7 Steven C. Martino, Rebecca L. Collins, Marc N. Elliot, Amy Strachman, David E. Kanouse, and Sandra H. Berry, "Exposure to Degrading Versus Nondegrading Music Lyrics and Sexual Behavior Among Youth," *Pediatrics* 118, no. 2 (2006): e430–41.

8 AP-MTV Digital Abuse Study, 2011.

9 Leslie Moonves, quoted in Michael Krasny, "Passing the Buck in Tinsel town," *Mother Jones,* January 1993.

10 See the report of the Internet Safety Technical Task Force as well as Larry Magid, "Net Threat to Minors Less Than Feared," CNET, January 13, 2009.

11 Ibid.

12 Neil Postman, interview on the *PBS News Hour,* 1996.

Chapter Five: Embracing the Positives of Digital Media

1 This story comes from my Common Sense colleague Shira Lee Katz, a very talented woman who got her PhD at Harvard Education School under Howard Gardner and who has been instrumental in developing our digital literacy curriculum.

2 Matt Richtel, "Growing Up Digital, Wired for Distraction," *New York Times,* November 21, 2011. See comments by Woodside High principal David Reilly.

3   See Mizuko Ito, Sonja Baumer, et al., *Hanging Out, Messing Around, and Geeking Out,* (Boston: MIT Press, 2009), Chapter 5.

4   Ibid., Chapter 6.

5   Ibid., Chapter 7, for a more detailed explanation of digital realities and their relation to career opportunities.

6   Ibid.

7   Ibid., pp. 38–76.

8   Interview with Howard Gardner, July 11, 2011, Stanford, California.

9   Eli Pariser, *The Filter Bubble: What the Internet Is Hiding from You* (New York: Penguin Press, 2011).

10   Interview with Eli Pariser, July 12, 2011, San Francisco, California.

11   Interview with Alec Ross, August 16, 2011, Washington, D.C. Sent by e-mail.

Chapter Six: Kids Are More Than Data Points

1   Interview with Ken Auletta, October 2011.

2   Ken Auletta, *The Highwaymen* (New York: Harcourt Brace and Co., 1997).

3   Reid Hoffman speaking at the Davos Annual Meeting 2010 (World Economic Forum).

Birth to Age Two

1   Dimitri A. Christakis, MD, MPH; Frederick J. Zimmerman, PhD; and Michelle M. Garrison, PhD, "Effect of Block Play on Language Acquisition and Attention in Toddlers: A Pilot Randomized Controlled Trial," *Archives of Pediatric and Adolescent Medicine* 161, no. 10 (2007): 967–71.

2   Harry Hoffman, "Raising a Little Genius," *Seattle Times,* April 25, 2008.

3   Frederick J. Zimmerman, PhD; Dimitri A. Christakis, MD, MPH, PhD; and Andrew N. Meltzoff, PhD, "Associations Between Media Viewing and Language Development in Children Under Age 2 Years," *Journal of Pediatrics,* August 7, 2007.

4   Alice Park, "Baby Einsteins: Not So Smart After All," *Time,* August 6, 2007.

5   Etienne Benson, "Toy Stories," *Observer,* Association for Psychological Science, December 2006.

6   Michael B. Robb, Rebekah A. Richert, and Ellen A. Wartella, University of California, Riverside, "Just a Talking Book? Word Learning from Watching

Baby Videos," *British Journal of Developmental Psychology* 27, Pt. 1 (March 2009): 27–45.

7   E. A. Vandewater, V. J. Rideout, E. A. Wartella, X. Huang, J. H. Lee, and M. S. Shim, Population Research Center, University of Texas, "Digital Childhood: Electronic Media and Technology Use Among Infants, Toddlers, and Preschoolers," *Pediatrics* 119, no. 5 (May 2007): e1006–15.

8   Padma Ravichandran and Brandl France de Bravo, MPH, "Young Children and Screen Time," National Research Center for Women and Families, June 2010.

9   Christakis, Zimmerman, and Garrison, "Effect of Block Play on Language Acquisition and Attention in Toddlers."

10 Zimmerman, Christakis, and Meltzoff, "Associations Between Media Viewing and Language Development in Children Under Age 2 Years"; Zimmerman and Christakis, "Children's Television Viewing and Cognitive Outcomes: A Longitudinal Analysis of National Data," *Archives of Pediatric & Adolescent Medicine* 159 (July 5, 2005): 619–25; D. A. Thompson and D. A. Christakis, "The Association between Television Viewing and Irregular Sleep Schedules among Children Less than 3 Years of Age," *Pediatrics* 116. no. 4 (October 2005): 851–56.

11 Jeana Lee Tahnk, "Making Your iPhone Even More Toddler-Friendly," Parenting.com, *February 15, 2011.*

Ages Three to Four

1   Dimitri Christakis and Frederick J. Zimmerman, "Violent Television Viewing During Preschool Is Associated with Antisocial Behavior During School Age," *Pediatrics* 120, no. 7 (2007): 993–99.

2   D. A. Christakis, F. J. Zimmerman, D. L. DiGuiseppe, and C. A. McCarty, "Early Television Exposure and Subsequent Attentional Problems in Children," *Pediatrics* 113, no. 4 (2004): 708–715.

3   Dimitri Christakis, "Smarter Kids Through Television: Debunking Myths Old and New," *Washington Post,* February 22, 2007.

4   Heather L. Kirkorian, Ellen A. Wartella, and Daniel R. Anderson, "Media and Young Children's Learning," *Future of Children* 18, no. 1 (Spring 2008): 39–61.

5   Dimitri A. Christakis, MD, MPH, and Frederick J. Zimmerman, PhD, "Violent Television Viewing During Preschool," *Pediatrics* 120, no. 5 (November 1, 2007), 993–99.

6   Kirkorian, Wartella, Anderson, "Media and Young Children's Learning," *Future of Children.*

7   Linda S. Pagani, Caroline Fitzpatrick, and Tracie A. Barnett of the Université de Montréal and its affiliated Sainte-Justine University Hospital Research Center, Canada, in collaboration with Eric Dubow of the University of Michigan, "Quebec Longitudinal Study of Child Development, Prospective Associations Between Early Childhood Television Exposure and Academic, Psychosocial, and Physical Well-being by Middle Childhood," *Archives of Pediatrics & Adolescent Medicine* 164, no. 5 (2010): 425–31.

8   Pamela Paul, "New Study Finds Gender Bias in Children's Books," *New York Times,* May 5, 2011.

9   Stephanie Pappas, "Preschoolers Already Think Thin Is Beautiful," Livescience.com, May 17, 2011.

Ages Five to Six

1   Amanda Gardner, "Kids' TV Time Linked to School Woes, Bad Habits," Health.com, May 3, 2010.

2   Ibid.

3   Ibid.

4   Lori Takeuchi, PhD, *Families Matter: Designing Media for a Digital Age*, The Joan Ganz Cooney Center at Sesame Workshop, June 2011, p. 14.

5   National Institute for Early Education Research, "Are New Media a Boon to Young Children's Education?" *Preschool Matters* 6, no. 2 (July/August 2008); Debra A. Lieberman, Maria Chesley Fisk, and Erica Biely, "Digital Games for Young Children Ages Three to Six: From Research to Design," *Computers in the Schools* 26, no. 4 (2009), 299–313.

6   Heather L. Kirkorian, Ellen A. Wartella, and Daniel R. Anderson, "Media and Young Children's Learning," *Future of Children* 18, no. 1 (Spring 2008): 39–61.

7   Texas Education Agency, *Evaluation of the Texas Technology Immersion Pilot: Final Outcomes for a Four-Year Study (2004–05 to 2007–08)*, January 2009.

8   Kirkorian, Wartella, and Anderson, "Media and Young Children's Learning."

9   Jay Blanchard and Terry Moore, "The Digital World of Young Children: Impact on Emergent Literacy," Pearson Foundation, March 1, 2010.

10 E. A. Vandewater, V. Rideout, E. A. Wartella, X. Huang, J. H. Lee, and M. Shim, "Digital Childhood: Electronic Media Use Among Infants, Toddlers and Preschoolers," *Pediatrics*.

11 Sharon Hayes; Stacey Tantleff-Dunn, "Am I Too Fat To Be a Princess?" *British Journal of Developmental Psychology* 28, no. 2 (2010): 413–26.

Ages Seven to Eight

1   Aviva Lucas Gutnick et al., *Always Connected: The New Digital Media Habits of Young Children,* The Joan Ganz Cooncy Center at Sesame Workshop, March 2011.

2   Victoria J. Rideout, Ulla G. Foehr, and Donald F. Roberts, *Generation M2: Media in the Lives of 8- to 18-Year-Olds,* Kaiser Family Foundation, January 2010.

3   Gutnick et al., *Always Connected: The New Digital Media Habits of Young Children.*

4   Joshua Brustein, "McDonald's Makes Subtle Play for Children Online," *New York Times,* April 20, 2011.

5   Lori Takeuchi, *Families Matter: Designing Media for a Digital Age.*

6   Belinda Goldsmith, "Children Use Web to Watch Videos, Look Up 'Sex,'" Reuters, August 12, 2009.

Ages Nine to Ten

1   Victoria J. Rideout, Ulla G. Foehr, and Donald F. Roberts, *Generation M2: Media in the Lives of 8- to 18-Year-Olds,* Kaiser Family Foundation, January 2010.

2   Aviva Lucas Gutnick et al., *Always Connected: The New Digital Media Habits of Young Children,* The Joan Ganz Cooney Center at Sesame Workshop, March 2011.

3   Growing Up with Media study, Internet Solutions for Kids, Johns Hopkins University, and the Centers for Disease Control and Prevention, March 2007.

4   Rideout et al., *Generation M2: Media in the Lives of 8- to 18-Year-Olds.*

5   Monica Heger, "Preteens and Glowing Screens," *Scientific American,* January 25, 2011.

Ages Eleven to Twelve

1 Cyberbullying 411.org, 2007.
2 Survey by Cliff Nass and Roy Pea, Stanford University, presented at Digital Media and Learning Conference, March 2011.
3 Nielsen, 2010.
4 Catherine Smith, "Facebook Removes 20,000 Underage Users Every Day," Huffington Post, March 23, 2011.
5 White House conference, "Overview of Cyberbullying."
6 Norton Canada Cyberbullying Survey, May 2011.
7 Ibid.

Ages Thirteen to Fifteen

1 Amanda Lenhart, "Teens, Cell Phones, and Texting," PEW Internet and American Life Project, April 20, 2011.
2 T. C. Liu, R. A. Desai, S. Krishnan-Sarin, D. A. Cavallo, and M. N. Potenza, "Problematic Internet Use and Health in Adolescents: Data from a High School Survey in Connecticut," *Journal of Clinical Psychiatry* 72 (2011): 836–45.
3 Dimitri A. Christakis, Megan M. Moreno, Lauren Jelenchick, Mon T. Myaing, and Chuan Zhou, "Problematic Internet Usage in U.S. College Students: A Pilot Study," *BMC Medicine* 22 (June 2011).
4 Liu, Desai, Krishnan-Sarin, Cavallo, and Potenza, "Problematic Internet Use," 836–845.
5 Loreal Lynch, "How Facebook Is Reshaping College Admissions," Schools.com, April 6, 2011.
6 Victoria J. Rideout, Ulla G. Foehr, and Donald F. Roberts, *Generation M2: Media in the Lives of 8- to 18-Year-Olds*, Kaiser Family Foundation, January 2010.

Conclusion

1 Shayndi Rice and Julia Angwin, "Facebook 'Unfair' on Privacy." *Wall Street Journal,* November 30, 2011.

Index

Index

brain: children under two, 99–100; digital anxiety and depression, 31–33, 44; impact of digital technology on, 36–38; importance of media time-outs, 35, 39–41; impulse control, 9–10, 31–32, 37–38, 74–75, 155–56, 171; plasticity of, 37; prefrontal cortex, 37–38

Brill, Julie, 60–61

Brin, Sergei, 62

Brooks, David, 67

Brown, Stephanie, 43

bullying. *see* cyberbullying

California, 72, 79

Call of Duty, 10, 43, 142, 145

caregivers, 106, 109, 123, 135

Carr, Nicholas, 37

Cartoon Network, 156, 165

Cator, Karen, 79

cell phones. *see also* smartphones: addiction to, 45; cyberbullying and, 30–31; driving and, 24, 41–43; impact on children, 7, 8; number owned, 7; prepaid phones *versus* smartphones, 151–52, 159; publishing and distribution opportunities, 86; texting capabilities, 164

Chambers, John, 93

cheating, 163, 171–72

CheatMasters, 146

childhood as "sequence of revealed secrets" (Postman), 12–13, 66, 68, 75

Christakis, Dimitri, 9–10, 37, 38, 44, 100, 108, 174

Clementi, Tyler, 29

Clinton, Hillary, 84

Club Penguin, 130, 132, 137, 138, 145

Cohen, Jared, 84

collaboration skills, 14, 80–81, 168

Columbine High School (Littleton, Colorado), 70

Common Sense Media, 2–3, 14, 28–30, 32–35, 48, 62–65, 67, 69, 79; anti-cyberbullying campaigns, 30; digital citizenship and literacy education, 15–16, 30, 34–35, 74, 80–81, 94, 163; legislative initiatives, 32, 62–63, 71–72; partnerships with Google, 49; privacy concerns, 55; ratings and age appropriateness, 108, 118, 121, 136

Compare People app, 6

compulsion. *see* addiction

content filters, 121–22, 126, 135–36, 148–50, 161–62

cookies, 60

Cook, Tim, 93

COPPA (Children's Online Privacy Protection Act). *see* legislation

Craigslist, 5

Create a Comic, 131

creativity, 79, 81–82, 165–66

critical-thinking skills, 15–16, 34, 69, 165

Crown, Susan, 81

Cut the Rope app, 117, 137

cyberbullying, 5–6, 9, 11, 26, 29–31, 52–53, 74, 158, 159, 163, 164–65, 169–70, 177

Cyrus, Miley, 68

Danner, John, 79

Daring Game for Girls, 143

data aggregation, 47, 49, 50, 57, 89

deductive reasoning, 80–81

democracy, 84–86, 92

depression, 31–33, 44, 169, 174

Index

Google, 6, 50, 84, 91, 117; impact on brains, 37, 40–41; news personalization trend, 86; plan to digitize all books, 89; privacy and, 47–49, 58, 59, 62, 176–77; Street View mapping vehicles, 58

Google Plus, 5, 30, 54

Gowalla, 177–78

Grand Theft Auto series, 70–71, 142

Guitar Hero, 142

hacking, 53, 58–59

"hanging out" online, 83–84

health problems, 109, 118, 124, 127, 131

hidden messages, 115

High Tech Charter School (San Diego), 79

Hoffman, Reid, 91

homework assignments, 81

Honesty Box app, 5–6, 170

Hughes, Chris, 85

identity development, 24–26, 56

Illinois, 72

impulse control, 9–10, 31–32, 37–38, 74–75, 155–56, 171

instant messaging (IMs), 8, 34, 44, 157–58

intellectual property, 89

Internet: browser controls, 121–22, 125–26, 135–36, 150, 161–62; X-rated websites, 13, 16–17, 69–70, 161–62

interruption technologies, 38, 40–41

iPad, 58, 94, 116, 136

iPhone, 58, 59, 80, 94

Iran, 84

Ito, Mizuko, 83

iTunes, 59, 127, 128, 139, 146, 172

Kaiser Family Foundation, 70

Kidzui browser, 126, 135–36, 150

Kiki Kannibal, 66–67

Kilbourne, Jean, 27

Klein, Joel, 79

language acquisition, 100, 102

Lanier, Jaron, 25, 49

legislation, 32, 62–63, 71–72; Children's Online Privacy Protection Act (COPPA), 25, 51, 60–61, 88–89, 92; Children's Television Act of 1990, 93; "Do Not Track Kids" bill, 62–63

Leibowitz, Jon, 61

Levine, Michael, 81

Lifeline! app, 103

"Like" button (Facebook), 5, 54

Line Surfer app, 125

LinkedIn, 5, 91

listening skills, 42, 120

location-sharing services, 177–78

Loopt, 11–12, 49, 177–78

MacArthur Foundation Digital Media and Learning Initiative, 79

malware, 139

Manhunt, 71

manual dexterity, 110–11

marketing, 11–12

Martha Speaks, 120

McDonald's, 127, 131

McLuhan, Marshall, 36

McWorld, 131, 132–33

media creep, 109–10

media-free times, 2, 23–24, 35, 39–41, 105, 125, 141, 149, 152, 162, 178

Meet New People app, 172

memory, 35, 39–41

"messing around" online, 83

Discussion Questions for Parents and Teachers

Parent to Parent

1. Did this book change the way you think about the role of technology and the Internet in your kids' lives? If so, how?
2. Harvard professor Howard Gardner speaks about the "epochal change" in the way we communicate and interact with one another. What do you think are the benefits of technology, especially when it comes to kids and family life? What are the drawbacks or losses in your opinion?
3. Which aspects of "RAP"—relationships, attention/addiction problems, and privacy—worry you most as a parent? Do you have personal examples or experiences that illustrate your concerns?
4. At the end of his Introduction, Jim stresses that parents need to talk with their children, limit their access to media, and stay involved in their lives. Which is the most important to you? Which is the most challenging? What are some initial steps you can take in your own family?
5. In this era of constant connectivity, have you found that technology detracts from interpersonal relationships? If so, how?

6. Do you find that technology affects the way you connect and relate to your child? Does it affect how your child relates to other children?

7. Do you agree that digital multitasking can lead to attention problems? What are some personal examples from your life or your child's?

8. During the teenage years, kids start forming their identities. Do you think "presentation anxiety" and the self-absorbed nature of social media affect the way your child is experimenting with his or her sense of identity? How is that different from when you were a teen?

9. Many kids and teens shy away from talking to their parents about digital dramas. Why do you think that is? How can parents present themselves as reliable, go-to resources for their kids?

10. As a parent, how can you encourage your child to self-reflect before he or she self-reveals? How can you help your child understand that there is no "eraser" button on the Internet and that digital footprints are permanent and persistent?

11. On page 48, Jim reveals some profound statistics from Common Sense Media about kids' attitudes toward privacy. How do your child's experiences relate? What are some ways you can begin a dialogue about these privacy issues with your child?

12. In this Wild West digital landscape, what kind of code for ethics and social responsibility should there be? Who should be accountable? Who should be responsible for the public interest?

13. Chapter 5 begins with Kranzberg's First Law of Technology: "Technology is neither good nor bad, nor is it neutral." What does Kranzberg mean? Do you agree or disagree? Why is digital reality so full of gray areas?

14. In the second half of the book, "Parenting 2.0: Top Common Sense Tips," which passages did you find insightful or noteworthy? Which were surprising or shocking? Which questions made you pause? Which recommendations do you think you will act upon?

15. As a parent, what are the implications for you now that you've read the book? What have you learned? What issues do you plan to tackle? What solutions have you devised?

16. In what ways can parents become role models for healthy digital-and-mobile-media use? What can you do in your own family?

Teachers to Students

1. How do you think your daily life would change if you took a time-out from all technology and media for a week? What changes would be welcomed? What might be some drawbacks? How could you adapt?

2. How can you help your peers become more aware of the fact that there is no "eraser" button for the information they put online? When it comes to your own digital footprint, what have been some of the harder lessons that you have learned?

3. How can technology increase young people's civic engagement? How are you able to participate in political and social initiatives more readily?

4. Mark Zuckerberg, CEO of Facebook, often speaks of "changing social norms" when it comes to perceptions of privacy. Reid Hoffman, founder of LinkedIn, claims that today's privacy concerns tend to be "old people issues." How do you view the notion of privacy, both from a legal and ethical stance? Do you worry about how companies use aspects of technology like geo-tracking and preference tracking to gather personal information about you?

5. Some say that today's generation is growing up too fast. Do you agree or disagree? Who are today's most recognizable role models? How do media introduce and present such role models nowadays? How do you discern between what is fact and what is fantasy online?

6. In what ways do you think boys and girls use digital media differently (if at all)? Why do you think these differences in behaviors exist?

7. In what ways can parents become role models for healthy digital and mobile media use? What could they do to make themselves more approachable as go-to resources?

8. Recent studies have raised concerns around digital depression. What are some of your health concerns when it comes to your current media diet? Do you see any consequences of digital multitasking in your daily life?

9. (Find your students' age group in "Part II: Parenting 2.0" and share with them Jim's tips about "What Parents Need to Know.") Do you agree or disagree with Jim's description of your age group? Which tips for parents do you think are the most valuable? Would you add any tips to the list?

10. What are the positive aspects of social network sites? What are the negative aspects? In your opinion, at what age does someone become "old enough" to have an account on a social network site? Why?

11. There has been a lot of attention around the topic of cyberbullying. What can you, as an individual or a peer group, do to stand up to cyberbullying and digital abuse?

12. Do you have family rules about what, when, and how much media you consume? If so, what are they? How are they enforced? How could you help your family create a well-balanced media diet?